LANGUAGE IN EDUCATION: THEORY AND PRACTICE

37

Discourse Analysis and Second Language Teaching

Claire J. Kramsch

Published by
Center for Applied Linguistics

Prepared by

ERIC® Clearinghouse on Languages and Linguistics

 This publication was prepared with funding from
the National Institute of Education, U.S.
Department of Education under contract no.
400-77-0049. The opinions expressed in this
report do not necessarily reflect the positions
or policies of NIE or ED.

Kramsch, Claire J.
   Discourse analysis and second language
teaching.

   (Language in education ; 37)
   Bibliography: p.
   1. Language and languages--Study and
teaching. 2. Discourse analysis. I. Title.
II. Series.
P53.K72   401'.41   81-38548
ISBN 0-87281-158-1   AACR2

LANGUAGE IN EDUCATION: THEORY AND PRACTICE

ERIC (Educational Resources Information Center) is a nationwide network of information centers, each responsible for a given educational level or field of study. ERIC is supported by the National Institute of Education of the U.S. Department of Education. The basic objective of ERIC is to make current developments in educational research, instruction, and personnel preparation more readily accessible to educators and members of related professions.

ERIC/CLL. The ERIC Clearinghouse on Languages and Linguistics (ERIC/CLL), one of the specialized clearinghouses in the ERIC system, is operated by the Center for Applied Linguistics. ERIC/CLL is specifically responsible for the collection and dissemination of information in the general area of research and application in languages, linguistics, and language teaching and learning.

LANGUAGE IN EDUCATION: THEORY AND PRACTICE. In addition to processing information, ERIC/CLL is also involved in information synthesis and analysis. The Clearinghouse commissions recognized authorities in languages and linguistics to write analyses of the current issues in their areas of specialty. The resultant documents, intended for use by educators and researchers, are published under the title Language in Education: Theory and Practice.* The series includes practical guides for classroom teachers, extensive state-of-the-art papers, and selected bibliographies.

The material in this publication was prepared pursuant to a contract with the National Institute of Education, U.S. Department of Education. Contractors undertaking such projects under Government sponsorship are encouraged to express freely their judgment in professional and technical matters. Prior to publication, the manuscript was submitted to the American Council on the Teaching of Foreign Languages for critical review and determination of professional competence. This publication has met such standards. Points of view or opinions, however, do not necessarily represent the official view or opinions of either ACTFL or NIE. This publication is not printed at the expense of the Federal Government.

This publication may be purchased directly from the Center for Applied Linguistics. It also will be announced in the ERIC monthly abstract journal Resources in Education (RIE) and will be available from the ERIC Document Reproduction Service, Computer Microfilm International Corp., P.O. Box 190, Arlington, VA 22210. See RIE for ordering information and ED number.

For further information on the ERIC system, ERIC/CLL, and Center/Clearinghouse publications, write to ERIC Clearinghouse on Languages and Linguistics, Center for Applied Linguistics, 3520 Prospect St., N.W., Washington, D.C. 20007.

---

*From 1974 through 1977, all Clearinghouse publications appeared as the CAL·ERIC/CLL Series on Languages and Linguistics. Although more papers are being added to the original series, the majority of the ERIC/CLL information analysis products will be included in the Language in Education series.

CONTENTS

What is this?
This is a book.
Good! Where is the book?
It is on the table.

These are correct English sentences. They are correct in
their grammar and in their usage. Yet the facts that (1) it is
obviously a book the teacher is pointing to and (2) the book is
lying on the table, visible to everyone, make it extremely
unnatural for the teacher to ask these questions. The students
give a response that satisfies the teacher, because they take
this rightly as a grammatical exercise and not as a conversational exchange.

Usually a question such as "What is this?" is either a
request for information ("What is this?"--"I don't know," or
"This is our new textbook"), or a request for a definition
("What is this?"--"It is a new textbook for teaching English
built around a functional-notional syllabus"), or else an
expression of surprise or disapproval ("What is this?" said
while pointing to a book chewed up by the dog). Here, in this
particular classroom context, the function of the question is
clearly to have the students just name the object as a "book"
(rather than a livre or a Buch) and really means "Give me the
English word for...." If most of the questions and answers
exchanged in the traditional language classroom pertain to the
formal aspects of the language (vocabulary, grammar, syntax),
then most of the skills developed by the students are grammatical, not conversational. Grammar is concerned with the formal
properties of the language, conversation or discourse with its
functional properties--with what the speaker uses the language
for. Although formed of grammatically correct sentences, most
of the exchanges in language classes are highly unnatural in
terms of discourse rules.

The concept of communicative competence, which has recently
become so influential in language teaching, has resulted in a
new emphasis on the nature of interaction and the rules of
discourse. Concentrating on the formal features of language,
generations of language teachers have attempted to develop
"speaking skills" by drilling syntactically correct sentences
into their students. The disappointment at the resulting lack
of conversational ability (Valette 1973, Rivers 1973) has
shifted the interest from studies on the structure of language
to studies on social interaction, on the meaning of utterances,
and on the functions of speech. Since Dell Hymes' seminal paper
on communication (1964), language researchers distinguish "what
is said" by the language from "what is done" by the language

(Labov 1972) and are interested in "exploring the functions of language" (Halliday 1973). As Firth had said as early as 1935, "Conversation is much more of roughly prescribed ritual than most people think....It is in conversation that we shall find the key to a better understanding of what language really is and how it works."

Conversational analysts such as the sociologists Sacks, Schegloff, and Jefferson, philosophers like Austin, Searle, and Grimes, and the linguists Halliday, Widdowson, Sinclair, and Coulthard are providing a foundation for a more effective approach to the teaching of language. This paper will explore how recent advances in sociolinguistics and discourse analysis lead us to re-examine the respective roles and privileges of teacher and students engaged in verbal interaction and how verbal behavior can be changed or acquired for greater conversational competence on the part of the students.

NATURAL DISCOURSE

One of the fundamental aims of discourse analysis is to discover the rules for the production of coherent verbal interaction. To use Widdowson's terms (1973), "Whereas grammarians are concerned with rules of usage which are exemplified in sentences, discourse analysts study rules of use which describe how utterances perform social acts. Sentences combine to form texts and the relations between sentences are aspects of grammatical cohesion; utterances combine to form discourse and the relations between them are aspects of discourse coherence." Only the first of the following examples is a cohesive text, but both examples are coherent discourse.

(1) A: Can you go to Frankfurt tomorrow?
     B: No, I can't.
(2) A: Can you go to Frankfurt tomorrow?
     B: Lufthansa pilots are on strike.

Rules of discourse cannot be expressed in grammatical terms; indeed, the linguistic form of the utterance is almost irrelevant. What is structurally important is the social act it performs, i.e., its linguistic function (here, for example, declining an invitation to go to Frankfurt). This functional level of discourse, which exists between grammar and content, regulates any verbal interaction and has to be explored if one is to understand what goes on between speaker and hearer.

Speech Acts

The philosopher of language J.L. Austin (1962) was one of the first to study meaning and reference rather than formal

2

structure. He first focused his attention on a group of sentences that he labelled "performatives," in which the saying of the
words constitutes the performing of an action. For instance, in
saying "I name this ship the Queen Elizabeth," the speaker is
not describing what he is doing, nor stating that he is doing
it, but is actually performing the action of naming the ship.
(It is by saying the words that one performs the action.) He
then noticed that the concept of performative utterances, of
doing something by saying something, had a more general application. He demonstrated that in fact all utterances are performative and that in "issuing an utterance," a speaker can perform
three acts simultaneously: a "locutionary" act, which is the
act of saying something in the full sense of "say"; an "illocutionary" act, which is an act performed in saying something; and
a "perlocutionary" act, the act performed by or as a result of
saying.

For example, the utterance "The ice over there is thin" is
not only a statement, an act of saying something, it is also a
warning, i.e., it has a meaning that goes beyond the locutionary
act of merely saying something. It performs the "illocutionary"
act of warning. Moreover, since this utterance is intended to
elicit a change in the listener--to make him think, become, or
do something (here, to become alarmed)--this utterance is also a
"perlocutionary" act. The perlocutionary act is the causing of
a change in the mind of the listener, so that he becomes alarmed,
convinced, deterred, etc.

John Searle (1969) further explored the notion of illocutionary acts. However, unlike Austin, Searle puts the illocutionary force of an utterance in the listener's interpretation
of the utterance, not in the intention of the speaker. By
introducing the hearer as an important element in discourse
operations, Searle prepared the way for research in conversational analysis. Moreover, he distinguished between two types
of rules that govern the linguistic realization of illocutionary
acts: the regulative and the constitutive.

Regulative rules are concerned with conditions in the occurrence of certain forms of behavior. All interaction has regulative rules, usually not explicitly stated. Constitutive rules
define the behavior itself. Regulative rules govern the initial
exchange of greetings between speakers; they control who chooses
the topic to speak about, who interrupts whom, how and when; and
they regulate the turn taking, the negotiating for understanding, and all the other tactical operations that occur during a
verbal exchange. Constitutive rules control the way in which a
given utterance of a given form is heard as realizing a given
illocutionary act. They determine which verbal and nonverbal
behavior must be used by the speaker if he or she wants to be
understood as promising something, issuing a warning, or giving
an order. Discourse analysis is concerned with both types of
rules, for they form the basis of verbal interaction.

Pragmatics

The influence of the speech act theories of Austin and
Searle is evident in all aspects of present-day research on spoken discourse. They are behind the growing interest among linguists in the relationship between the grammatical rules that
generate sentences and the pragmatic rules that govern their
use. They explain the current high interest in pragmatics,
sociolinguistics, and applied logic. Pragmatics (Gordon and
Lakoff 1971; Oller 1970, 1973; Fillmore 1972) is the study of
the relationship between sentence meaning (what is literally
said), manner of speaking (intonation, pauses, fluency, etc.),
context of speaking (who, to whom, where, when); and utterance
meaning (intended illocutionary act). When applied to language
learning, it searches to define which illocutionary acts are
available in the language, which strategies are necessary to
perform each illocutionary act, and which are the appropriate
contexts for using a given strategy.

Pragmatics has three claims with regard to language learning: (1) every language has available roughly the same set of
illocutionary acts; (2) every language has available roughly the
same set of strategies for performing a given illocutionary act;
(3) languages differ significantly with respect to both when a
certain illocutionary act ought to be performed and, if so, with
what strategy (Fraser 1979).

To describe the phenomenon "speech" in its whole context,
Hymes (1971) has proposed "a second descriptive science of language," the ethnography of speaking, the aim of which is to
describe and systematize the interpretive rules used by members
of a given speech community. Sociolinguists involved in
researching these rules call themselves ethnomethodologists;
they are concerned not simply with language structure but with
language use, with "rules of speaking...(i.e.) the ways in which
speakers associate particular modes of speaking, topics or message forms with particular settings and activities" (Hymes
1972a). For every speech "event," Hymes recommends that the
ethnographer initially provide data on structure, topic, participants, setting, purposes, and channel of communication.

Ethnomethodology has had an impact on scholars in other disciplines, working for different purposes on English conversation. It has made them more aware of the importance in conversation of the psychological setting, of the roles and status of
each participant, of the key "tone, manner or spirit" in which
the conversation takes place, of the choice of topic, and of the
rituals of rule breaking.

Research in pragmatics has revived the interest of linguists
in the work of logicians and rhetoricians such as Baird, Perelman, and Grimes, and in the Aristotelian spirit of forensic and
deliberative speaking. If discourse is indeed a "mode of intervention on others" (Portine 1978), one of the major functions of

language is the argumentative function, and a major criterion of communicative competence is speech effectiveness. The logical presentation and organization of ideas is one condition for effective speaking.

Discourse studies are now being undertaken in many languages. Although we are still far from having a grammar of discourse, many of the existing studies on the relationship between speaker and hearer in public speaking (Grimes 1975, Perelman 1970), on patterns of inquiry (Baird 1965), on units of hierarchy within discourse (Grimes 1975), on specific discourse functions, e.g., persuading, convincing (Perelman 1970), disagreeing (Debyser 1978), and apologizing (Fraser 1979) can be of great value to researchers in language teaching. The theory is too broad to be synthesized here, but I will examine later some of the practical applications that have already been proposed for the teaching of foreign languages.

Natural Discourse and First Language Acquisition

Research in child language acquisition has also changed its focus to a concern with pragmatics and interaction. Dore (1974, 1975) shows that children's utterances cannot be described in purely grammatical terms, but that they are in fact realizations of one of nine primitive speech acts: labelling, repeating, answering, requesting (action), requesting (answer), calling, greeting, protesting, and practicing. Halliday (1973) suggests that the only way to interpret the child's early (9-19 months) communication system is in the following six _functional_ categories: instrumental (the "I Want" function), regulatory (the "Do as I Tell You" function), interactional (the "Me and You" function), personal (the "Here I Come" function), heuristic (the "Tell Me Why" function), and imaginative (the "Let's Pretend" function). To these microfunctions are added in adulthood three macrofunctions: the representational, the interpersonal, and the textual.

Interestingly enough, both Dore and Halliday omit from their list of children's speech acts or functional categories any type of statement or assertion. Halliday notes that the absence of such speech acts is not surprising, since the idea that one can use language to convey information not known to the hearer is a sophisticated one. In fact, he adds, "stating is the only use of language in a function that is definable solely by reference to language." Language teachers will want to draw conclusions from that fact in view of the inordinate amount of stating, describing, and relating that is traditionally practiced in classrooms.

Most of the work in the acquisition of discourse has been concerned with examining how the child produces and interprets individual speech acts; it deals mostly with the acquisition of Searle's "constitutive" rules of discourse. However, some linguists are beginning to study how the child learns to converse. Studies on the conversational structure or regulative rules of interaction between children were conducted by Keenan (1975) with monthly videotapes of her twin sons, who were 2.9 years old at the beginning of the research and 3.8 at the end. Contrary to Piaget's observations (1926) that even at the age of 5 or 6, children tend not to address their speech to a copresent listener, the evidence from Keenan's children showed the great importance the twins attached to relevance and turn taking.

Keenan and Klein (1975) identified five types of acknowledgment or relevant response: basic acknowledgment (direct repetition), affirmation (explicit agreement), denial (negation or opposition), matching (claim to be performing a similar action), and extension (new predication to previous speaker's topic). The listener is expected to produce one of these acknowledgments; if he doesn't, the speaker may repeat his assertion until it is acknowledged. Keenan and Klein noticed that children rarely repeat sentences for repetition's sake, as students are asked to do in a classroom. Their repetitions are discursive operations: they struggle to create coherent and cohesive discourse utterance by utterance, using requests for clarification, comments, and acknowledgment as their main strategies.

Garvey (1975), working with slightly older children, notes that by the age of 5-1/2 the children have mastered most of the complexities of conversational structure: getting attention, taking turns, making relevant utterances, nominating and acknowledging topics, ignoring and avoiding topics, priming topics ("See that hammer there? Yeah. Hand it to me"), and requesting clarification. "It seems reasonable to suggest that learning to produce discourse can be understood as learning to perform the component behaviors which contribute to the successful execution of speech acts, learning the relative order of these behaviors, and learning the appropriate distribution of roles which the alternating turns require."

In her interesting study of the solicited and unsolicited query, Garvey (1977) even shows that learning to talk is in fact learning how to interact.

Solicited query: You know what?
                        What?
                        This is a nice place.

Unsolicited query: This is a nice place.
                        What?
                        This is a nice place.
                        What's a nice place? this room?
                        Yup.
                        Oh, yeah.

This important conversational skill is well learned by the time speech is fluent, that is, by about 3 to 3-1/2 years of age. The interpersonal function of solicited queries appears to be the promotion of mutual attention or rapport, that of unsolicited queries the maintenance of mutual understanding. "It is certainly not a conversational refinement that is learned sometime after the basic syntactic features of the linguistic code are learned. On the contrary, it seems to be acquired as part of learning to talk and to listen and to talk."

It might even be that the syntactic structures of speech grow out of the discourse structure itself. Scollon's work (1973) on children shows that the "horizontal" structures produced by the child develop out of the "vertical" structures of the interaction with other children or with adults.

> Child: Hiding.
> Adult: Hiding? What's hiding?
> Child: Balloon.

When adults ask for more information on the topic by means of questions, they ask for a syntactic constituent to fill out the construction. What children learn is conversation, and the syntax grows out of the necessities of the conversation. "This suggests," says Scollon, "that discourse structure is at the heart of sentence structure from the beginning of its development."

If we re-examine in the light of this research Halliday's distinction between micro- and macrofunctions of language, it seems that we should no longer consider the interpersonal and textual macrofunctions as a later development, an adult addition to the "simpler" functions used by the child. Rather, they seem to be the very vehicle through which the microfunctions can be exercised. Preceding the lexical, morphological, and syntactic choices made by the speaker/hearer to fulfill any of the microfunctions, we have a grid of interpersonal and textual functions that operate within the interactional context of language acquisition.

Thus, in children as in adults, "the total speech act in the total speech situation is the only actual phenomenon which, in the last resort, we are engaged in elucidating" (Austin 1962). The verbal communicative competence that develops takes place concurrently on the grammatical level of the sentence, on the pragmatic level of the speech act, and on the discourse level of the regulative strategy. As Goodwin (1975) noted, "An actual utterance cannot properly be viewed only as a more or less flawed production by a speaker employing his or her grasp of the rules of sentence construction. Instead it must be seen as an interactional object, subject not only to syntactic and semantic constraints in the narrow sense but also to the properties of speaker-hearer interaction."

Moving away from Chomsky's too narrow definition of compe-

7

tence, i.e., the ideal speaker-hearer's knowledge of grammaticality (Chomsky 1957) to the broader concept of communicative competence (Hymes 1972b), i.e., "the speaker's ability to produce appropriate utterances, not grammatical sentences," we can thus identify three major aspects of this communicative competence: (1) a grammatical competence necessary to make oneself understood (locutionary acts), (2) a pragmatic competence (illocutionary acts), and (3) a discursive competence (conversational acts).

Natural Discourse of Native Adults

Research on this third level of communication has been done mainly by conversational analysts and applied logicians. Until very recently, most of the advances in conversational analysis have been made by a small group of sociologists: Sacks, Schegloff, and Jefferson. Their descriptions of "conversational mechanisms" provide detailed evidence of the high degree of structuring in everyday conversation. Although they work with conversational materials not out of a special interest in language but because they want to study details of social interactions in a "rigorous, empirical and formal way," their findings have interesting implications for the teaching of conversation in foreign language classrooms.

Turn Taking

Turn taking is one of the most important strategies of conversation. There is an underlying rule in most cultures that "at least and not more than one party talks at a time." Speakers have a range of possibilities for controlling the next turn. They can select the next speaker by naming or alluding to him or her, or they can "constrain" the next utterance but not select the next speaker (for example, by producing a question or a greeting that constrains the next speaker to produce an appropriate response or return greeting). Or they can select neither and leave it to one of the other participants to continue the conversation by volunteering.

Sacks et al. (1974) note that these selection techniques operate only utterance by utterance; there is no mechanism in conversation by which current speakers can select the speaker after next, unless it is themselves. In more formal speech situations such as classrooms, it is quite possible for the teacher, whose role assigns him or her extra authority, to select the speakers for several successive utterances.

One of the most important things for the next speaker is to know when the current speaker is finished and, therefore, when he or she can begin. Since it is always possible to add something to an apparently complete utterance, and speakers frequently do so, next speakers are concerned with recognizing

8

points of "possible completion." Such points are, for instance, ends of sentences, where speakers are particularly vulnerable. Indeed, as Coulthard (1977) notes, "the ability to come in as soon as a speaker has reached a possible completion requires a high degree of skill on the part of the participants; they need to be able both to analyze and understand an ongoing sentence in order to recognize when it is possibly complete, and also to produce immediately a relevant next utterance."

Silence between turns creates a problem, and participants feel that a silence is attributable usually to some intended next speaker. This puts a pressure not on the previous speaker to continue, but on potential next speakers to take the turn. There is a very low tolerance of silence between turns. If the next intended speakers do not begin almost at once, either the previous speakers will repeat their last utterance or ask a question, or the next speakers will indicate their intention to speak by "erm," "um," "mm," or an audible intake of breath and thereby incorporate the silence into their turn.

There are several techniques open to speakers who wish to continue speaking past a particular "possible completion" point. Sacks et al. (1974) mention "utterance incompletors" such as "but" or "however," which turn complete sentences into incomplete ones. Indeed, Ferguson (1975), after examining 11 hours of conversation, found that 28 percent of interruptions occurred after conjunctions. By using subordinators or even structuring in advance a fairly large unit of speech with such devices as "on the one hand,...on the other hand" or "I'd like to make two points: first,..." speakers can, if not totally guarantee the floor for themselves, at least force other speakers into a position where they must interrupt.

Moves

Conversational analysts are concerned with defining the size of the basic unit in conversation. Labov (1970, 1972), Sacks (1972), Schegloff (1968, 1972), and Jefferson (1972, 1973) use utterance or turn. Sinclair and Coulthard (1975) add a smaller unit, which they call move. A move can coincide with a turn, but in some cases, as in A's utterance below, one turn can contain two moves:

A: Can you tell me why do you eat all that food?
B: To keep you strong.
A: To keep you strong, yes, to keep you strong. Why do you want to be strong?

Conversation is structured by four major combinations of moves:

1. Chaining. "A person who has asked a question has...a reserved right to talk again, after the one to whom he has

addressed the question speaks. And in using this reserved right he can ask a question" (Sacks 1972). The example above is an illustration of this chaining rule and yields a discourse pattern rather characteristic of teacher talk in the classroom: Question - Answer - Question - Answer. Sinclair and Coulthard's further distinction of moves shows that the traditional pattern for teacher/pupil interaction is T - P - T, T - P - T, rather than T - P, T - P, T - P. Teachers use their "reserved" right to talk again after their first question has been answered, but in so doing, they perform in fact two moves: first comment, then question.

2. Insertion sequence

A:	I don't know where the--wh--this address (pause) is.	Q
B:	Well where do--which part of town do you live?	Q_1 ⎫ Insertion
A:	I live 410 East Lowden.	A_1 ⎬ sequence
B:	Well, you don't live very far from me.	A ⎭

An insertion sequence suggests to the speaker, "If you can answer this one, I can answer yours." It is often used, as in the case above, for clarification purposes, not for changing the topic.

3. Side sequence. This is generally a request for clarification that temporarily interrupts the flow of the conversation. Jefferson (1972) gives as an example children preparing for a game of tag.

Steven: One, two, three (pause), four, five, six (pause), eleven, eight, nine, ten.
Susan: Eleven, eight, nine, ten?
Steven: Eleven, eight, nine, ten.
Nancy: Eleven?
Steven: Seven, eight, nine, ten.
Susan: That's better.

This is also a good example of the "negotiation for meaning" that goes on between speakers and hearers. (I will refer to this later when we consider the applications for language learning.)

4. Tying.

A: Where was everybody last night?
B: Well, John and Lisa went to the movies.
C: Did they? I stayed at home, for once.

10

The fact that utterances and pairs of utterances are not isolated but tied to preceding utterances means that speakers must
understand what has gone before in order to produce a correctly
tied utterance. Sacks even argues that a speaker cannot <u>not</u> tie
if the conversation is to run smoothly. Tying fulfills two
functions: it ensures a cohesive exchange, and it shows that
the speaker has understood previous utterances.

Topic

A conversation that is progressing well drifts imperceptibly
from one topic to another, and speakers must constantly choose
what is suitable to "tell" in the course of a conversation.
This concept of "tellability" or newsworthiness is difficult to
apply to a particular item in a particular conversation, but it
is used by conversationalists all the time. Speakers who want
to change the topic have to justify their new choice of topic by
tying grammatically and topically what they want to say to what
has gone before. If their own topic is being changed by another
aggressive speaker, skillful speakers know how to reassert it by
using "skip-connecting," i.e., relating back to the next-to-last
utterance.

Equally important for the speakers is to know how to end
conversations. Speakers don't just stop talking. Conversations
always end when a topic has ended or other speakers have agreed
not to introduce any new topics. "Arriving at a point where a
closing sequence can begin requires a certain amount of work"
(Coulthard 1977). Speakers have to indicate verbally that they
have nothing further to add to the topic by using their turn to
produce markers such as "all right," "okay," "so," or "well."
This allows the next speaker the choice of either introducing an
entirely new topic or of adding to the first speaker's possible
preclosing sequence his or her own preclosing sequence. We have
here a "negotiation for ending" between the two speakers. (For
the three-phase closing ritual in German, see Jäger 1976b).

Although conversation analysis is still restricted to describing isolated features of conversation and still lacks the
explicitness and formalization necessary to relate forms to
functions in a more systematic way, it provides valuable insights into the uses of discourse, and forms a basis for future
developments in language teaching. For, indeed, the evidence
from first language acquisition and from naturally occurring
conversations between native adults shows that both children and
adults use a discourse model for interacting with one another.
Do learners of a second language behave the same way when using
this second language in natural situations?

Natural Discourse and Second Language Acquisition

Pairing five Spanish-speaking children (the youngest was
5.9, the oldest 6.11) with five English-speaking friends for

observation, Fillmore (1979) tracked the second language development (English) of the Spanish-speaking children over one school year, in order to discover "what social processes might be involved when children who need to learn a new language come into contact with those from whom they are to learn it--but with whom they cannot communicate easily." Her results show that to get proper input, i.e., language as it is used in social situations that make sense, the typical second language learner must "play an active role in inviting interaction from the speakers of the language and in maintaining contact once it is established." In order to manage the interaction, the learner needs some very special social skills, and these skills are at least as important as the cognitive skills for successful language learning. The strategies she observed in the successful learners parallel those observed in children learning their mother tongue: actively taking turns in the interaction by paying attention to what is going on, guessing at the topic on the basis of contextual information, stretching one's repertoires of expressions, focusing on important points, and cooperating with the other speaker for "repair" and understanding.

Using a discourse analysis point of view to study adults learning a second language in natural situations, Hatch (1978) was able to show that the adult learner also uses a discourse model as much as possible. This model is similar in some respects to that used by children learning their mother tongue. It includes capturing attention, priming the topic, nominating it, accepting it, and soliciting clarification. However, there are some differences. Because the discourse of adult-adult conversation is more abstract--relying much less on immediate environment than adult-child or child-child interactions--and because it can cover an incredibly wide range of topics, topic identification is much more difficult for adults.

As a result, adults use a "fine discrimination" model in which they can predict and steer the discourse topic by using priming questions. Once the topic of discourse is set, adult learners can form a grid for listening based on their knowledge of discourse possibilities within that topic. Without the grid, they would become lost in phonetic and syntactic detail and understand nothing. Thus, adults use a much larger array of strategies than children for predicting, checking, and matching.

Also, as Peck (1978) shows in her study of child-child discourse, since adults are more concerned about referential meaning, the character of their discourse is less playful, more informational, and contains more requests for clarification. Whereas children will just ignore a question or a topic if they do not feel like honoring it, adults will use time-holding devices such as rhetorical questions, repetitions, and linking strategies to return to an earlier point or to avoid the topic.

The use of a discourse model by both children and adults for the acquisition of language has wide implications for second language acquisition research. By observing the way learners "manage" the discourse in which or through which they learn, we can see how they "extend their cognitive control over their environment" (Kelly 1955). What Candlin and Breen call "negotiating, interpreting and expressing abilities" are management strategies that not only "encourage intake by allowing conversation" as Krashen (1978) suggests, but constitute the very process of learning itself (Candlin and Breen 1981). "The problem of learning is not merely one of determining how many or what kinds of reinforcements fix a response or how many non-reinforcements extinguish it, but rather how does the (learner) phrase the experience" (Kelly 1955).

CLASSROOM DISCOURSE

How are foreign language learners in the classroom given the opportunity to phrase (i.e., organize) their learning experience in terms of discourse management?

As in naturally occurring conversations, speakers in a classroom situation operate on three levels of structure, which Riley (1977) calls: (1) the formal structure, composed of a set of message-bearing elements (verbal, paralinguistic, nonverbal) and its grammatical and syntactic units of realization; (2) the illocutionary structure, composed of illocutionary forces or acts (inviting, agreeing, etc.); (3) the interactive structure, composed of interactional tactics, and classified according to their relative distribution and privileges of occurrence. The first two levels constitute the communicative level of the interaction. The third is the discursive level.

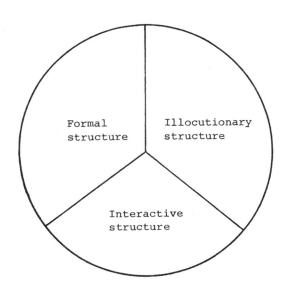

Students tend to identify all their linguistic problems as being those of "vocabulary, grammar, and idiom, whereas many are in fact communicative and discursive" (Riley 1976a). These problems have to do with "the ability to express the illocutionary force of an utterance as specified by its linguistic and situational context" (communicative competence) and with "the ability to organize and articulate the constituent content categories of the discourse in a comprehensible and acceptable way" (discursive competence). Their main difficulty is that of interacting effectively according to their role in the interaction.

The notion of "role" (Gremmo et al. 1977) has emerged from the studies on communicative interaction. Illocutionary acts as well as interactive and discursive acts are realizations of certain roles, i.e., the enactment of the privileges and duties of the speakers in a given situation. Studies of classroom interaction (Allen and Widdowson 1974, Gremmo et al. 1977, Sinclair and Coulthard 1975, Coulthard 1977, Johns 1974, Riley 1977) show that the illocutionary acts that teachers and students perform are part of their respective roles. While students traditionally restrict themselves to the illocutionary acts of repeating, practicing, and informing, ironically enough, it is the teachers who use the range of other functions that form communicative competence.

In addition to these overwhelming communicative privileges, which they can relinquish if they are skilled, teachers have discursive privileges that are equally overwhelming. In the traditional classroom context, their rights of address are exclusive: they and they alone can select the speakers and have control over who speaks next; they alone can interrupt; they alone choose the topic, i.e., "throw the discourse open." Since students only address the teacher, the teacher is the only one to produce opening and closing turns. These discursive features of classroom interaction would not be possible in other types of situations. This is why, according to Oller (1970), "the difficulty is not to teach second languages, but to teach them in classrooms." In addition to the contrast between the amount of teacher talk and that of student talk, there is an overwhelming contrast between teacher acts and student acts. Almost all teacher acts involve some form of control over the learner's behavior. "The teacher's task of classroom management is clearly reflected in his task of discourse management" (Gremmo et al. 1977).

Thirty seconds of classroom interaction are sufficient to illustrate the respective privileges and duties in the traditional classroom (Riley 1977):

T: Right,...the bottom of the page, then--whose turn is it? X?
X: Is my turn. What--
T: Is it my turn?
X: Is it my turn?

```
T:   Good.  Yes, I think it was.
X:   What means "the way"?
T:   Anyone?
Y:   Le chemin, montrer le chemin.
T:   Le chemin, right, good.
X:   "Can you tell me the way to Victoria Station, please?"
T:   Fine.  Z?
Z:   "Certainly.  It's down there, on the right."
```

There is evidence that a good deal of time is taken up by teachers with younger pupils in teaching them the discourse rules of the classroom and in getting them to recognize and respond appropriately to the teacher's signals. Later, students instinctively abide by these rules in all classroom situations. What are these discourse rules?

Over the past 15 years many researchers from a wide range of disciplines have studied the interaction of teacher and pupils in the classroom. Most of the descriptions they offer were motivated by pedagogic concerns. The systems developed by Bellack et al. (1966) and Sinclair and Coulthard (1975) are the most interesting for our purposes, because they categorize utterances in terms of discourse function rather than pedagogical function. This will enable us later to examine how the structural behaviors they identify can be applied to classroom interaction in a less traditionally "pedagogical" or teacher-centered setup.

Just as Sacks used the word turn for conversation, Bellack suggests that all classroom interaction can be described in terms of four moves:

1. Structuring. Structuring moves by the teacher serve to set the context by either launching or halting/excluding inter-action between students and teacher. For example, teachers will focus the attention of the class on a specific topic or problem to be discussed. Or they will summarize what has been said up to now (see reacting move below) and open up new avenues for discussion. Or they will cut a digression short and return to a previous point.

2. Soliciting. Moves in this category are intended to eli-cit an active verbal response on the part of the persons addressed or a cognitive response, e.g., encouraging persons addressed to attend to something. All questions are solicita-tions, as are commands and requests.

3. Responding. Students' answers to teachers' questions are classified as responding moves. Their function is to ful-fill the expectation of soliciting moves.

4. Reacting. These moves are occasioned by a structuring, soliciting, responding, or prior reacting move, but are not directly elicited by them. These moves serve to modify (by clarifying, synthesizing, or expanding) and/or to rate (positively or negatively) what has been said previously.

Bellack notes that "moves occur in classroom discourse in certain cyclical patterns or combinations which we designated teaching cycles. A (typical) teaching cycle begins either with a structuring or a soliciting move,...continues with a responding move by the student addressed, and ends with an evaluative reaction by the teacher." He identifies a total of 21 different structural cycles. "Styles of pedagogical discourse," he adds, "can be described in terms of cycle activity, percentage of teacher-initiated cycles, and distribution of cycle types."

Sinclair and Coulthard (1975) refined and expanded Bellack's system and devised a rank scale model of classroom interaction based on four major levels of discourse: the lesson, the transaction, the exchange, and the move. They distinguish among four categories of teaching acts at the "move" level: opening, answering, follow-up, and focusing. These four categories are subdivided into 21 discourse acts as follows:

Opening Moves: (1) marker (marks boundaries in the discourse); (2) starter (provides information about or directs attention to or thought toward an area); (3) elicitation (requests a linguistic response); (4) check (enables the teacher to ascertain whether the lesson is progressing successfully); (5) directive (requests a nonlinguistic response); (6) informative (provides information); (7) prompt (reinforces a directive or elicitation); (8) clue (provides additional information that helps students answer the elicitation); (9) cue (evokes a bid); (10) bid (signals a desire to contribute to the discourse); and (11) nomination (calls on or gives permission to a student).

Answering Moves: (1) acknowledge (shows that the initiation has been understood and the student intends to react); (2) reply (provides linguistic response which is appropriate to the elicitation); and (3) react (provides appropriate nonlinguistic response defined by the preceding directive).

Follow-up Moves: (1) accept (indicates that the teacher has heard or seen and that informative move, reply, or react move was appropriate); (2) evaluate (comments on the quality of the reply, react, or initiation moves); and (3) comment (exemplifies, expands, justifies, or provides additional information).

Framing and Focusing Moves: (1) metastatement (helps students see the structure of the lesson, helps them understand the purpose of the subsequent exchange and see where they are going); (2) conclusion (helps students see the structure of the lesson by summarizing what the preceding chunk of discourse was about); (3) loop (returns the discourse to the stage it was at before the student spoke, from where it can proceed normally); and (4) aside (instances where the teacher talks to himself or herself, not really addressed to the class).

Sinclair calls opening, answering, and follow-up moves "teaching moves"; framing and focusing are "boundary moves."

Sinclair and Coulthard make interesting observations concerning the respective control that teacher and pupils have on the conversation by managing the appropriate discourse moves. If this list is exhaustive for all types of discourse moves happening in classrooms, the number of discourse operations that are the privilege of the teacher would be enough to explain the consistent finding that teachers talk, on the average, for two-thirds of the talking time. Not only is the number of teacher acts versus pupils' acts remarkably high, but the complexity of teacher moves is also quite striking, as can be seen in the following short exchange:

> T: Can anyone have a shot, a guess at that one? (opening, elicit)
> S: Cleopatra. (answering move, reply)
> T: Cleopatra. (follow-up, accept)
> Good girl. (follow-up, evaluate)
> She was the most famous queen, wasn't she? (follow-up, comment)

The second move--the pupil's responding move--is far less complex than the teacher's follow-up moves. The teacher has to fit the reply with the ongoing discourse, take the information offered into the discourse (accept), assess its worth and relevance (evaluate) and add new related information (comment). Pupils can only participate in the discourse through the teacher by bidding for a turn, by replying to elicitations, reacting to directives, or acknowledging information. All the structuring, framing, focusing, mitigating, concluding, and commenting are the teacher's privilege.

A comparison of the rights and duties of the teacher in the traditional classroom and those of speakers in naturally occurring conversations shows that the classroom discourse of the teacher parallels quite closely that of interactional partners in natural conversations (see Tables 1a, 2a, 3a on pp. 23-26). The teacher's moves to open the interaction, to frame and focus, and to answer and follow up correspond almost exactly to the strategies necessary to sustain a natural conversation: turn taking, internal organization of the turn, and negotiation for understanding.

If learning a language is primarily learning how to manage one's discourse in the language, then management skills should be taught concurrently with the formal structures of speech and with the other communicative skills. Students should be taught to "speak like the teacher."

TEACHING NATURAL DISCOURSE IN THE CLASSROOM

Teachers eager to "decentralize" the learning experience of their students and to reduce the amount of teacher control on both the communicative and the discursive levels tend to adopt the role of seminar leaders and to offer their pupils the new role of seminar participants. This is a way of "removing the dominance of the teacher while preserving his accountability" (Jorstad 1974). Johns (1974) contrasts the two roles as follows:

Role of Teacher	Role of Seminar Leader
In linguistic control throughout the lesson, his obligations include: 1. Signalling the initiation and termination of different stages/activities of the lesson. 2. Initiation of exchanges 3. Control of turn taking 4. Giving appropriate feedback to acknowledge/evaluate responses. Hence highly structured interaction, describable in terms of a teacher-class dialogue	Most seminar leaders seem to undertake a degree of high-level organization (signalling and commenting on relationship of seminar to other teaching activities and probably on main stages of discussion); exercise of low-level organization (cf. 2, 3, 4 opposite) tends to be intermittent, the seminar leader preferring to intervene on this level only for "repair purposes." Intention is mostly to undertake as little low-level organization as possible and to set up a polylogue.

However, the more the teacher abandons the low-level organization of the interaction, the more that responsibility rests with the students. Control is "up for grabs." Students have to interrupt each other, take turns, choose to avoid the topic, react, evaluate, respond, etc. The more reserved or less proficient students fall prey to those who have better conversational management skills. There are at present extremely few language-teaching materials that could effectively teach them how to "behave appropriately" in this new decentralized situation.

Since Wilkins' (1972a) framework of a communicative notional syllabus was set forth, more and more material is becoming available to teach communicative verbal behaviors that were heretofore the restricted privilege of the teacher. In search of a "common core" to all Western European languages for the teaching of foreign languages to adults in the European Community, the Council of Europe identified basic categories of communicative functions and their linguistic realizations for the elementary (threshold) and more advanced levels.

Wilkins observes that "language learning has concentrated... in the use of language to report and describe" but claims that these two functions "are by no means the only ones that are important for the learner of a foreign language." The kinds of functions he has in mind and that are traditionally used by the teacher in the classroom are "judgment, approval, disapproval, suasion, prediction, greeting, sympathy, gratitude, flattery, hostility, information asserted, information sought," etc.[1] Although we are still far from having a complete communicatively structured syllabus--let alone textbooks built around it--many publications offer suggestions and even practical applications of the functional-notional approach to language learning.[2]

What is almost totally absent, however, is material to develop Riley's third level of competence: the interactive or discursive competence. The discursive features of speech are one aspect of "conversational ability" that is generally under-rated by students. They don't realize that the traditional pat-terns of classroom discourse are working against them as they try to develop conversational fluency. They have acquired dis-cursive competence in their mother tongue within its culturally appropriate rules of behavior, but as far as the foreign lan-guage is concerned, they have been exposed in the classroom to highly unusual or even deviant discourse patterns that have nothing in common either with the discourse patterns of their mother tongue or with those of the foreign language and culture.

Developing interactional competence means that the language student has to learn the key moves in the management of dis-course (Candlin 1976). These are turn taking, linking and expanding, negotiation, and repair. If teachers relinquish their privilege to prompt, direct, elicit, and nominate, it is up to the students/speakers themselves to prompt, constrain, and resist the intervention by other participants in the interac-tion. It is up to the speaker to make an appropriate interven-tion. For this, speakers have to learn how to signal to the other participants that they want to take the floor in support of or in opposition to the previous speaker or by steering the topic in another direction.

Here, different cultural patterns of aggressiveness have to be taken into consideration. For example, the American student used to the debate style of interaction, where each partner exposes his or her viewpoint without being interrupted, tends to wait for the previous speaker to be finished before taking the floor. French and German speakers favor the more argumentative type of discussion, whose goal, as Jäger (1976a) notes, is not just to ventilate ideas, but to clarify controversial points as they come up.

Thus, not only is it the responsibility of speakers to state their opinion as completely and explicitly as possible, but it is the right and the duty of listeners to try and interrupt them as soon as they perceive a controversial statement and are able to counter it. Learning a foreign language means learning these culturally different verbal behaviors.

By the time potential speakers are able to intervene, the conversation may have moved beyond the point that they wish to take up. Since the teacher has relinquished his or her privi-

lege of framing and focusing, it is up to the students to dis-
turb the linear sequence of the conversation and return to a
previous point. For this they have to learn how to handle the
side sequence by holding the "return point" in short-term memory
and mastering the linguistic means of cross-referring to that
point.

Another powerful skill to be learned by the student is the
metacomment. It is no longer the teacher who evaluates and
gives feedback, but the speaker who evaluates the previous
speaker's contribution with a retrospective metacomment
(accepting, evaluating, agreeing, disagreeing, fighting back) or
a prospective metacomment (signalling the rhetorical/logical
relationship of what is to come with what has gone before, e.g.,
using contrast, amplification, restriction, generalization,
exemplification, explanation, exploration of causes, consequences, or alternatives).

If we think of a conversation as a situation where participants compete for the floor and negotiate for understanding,
speakers need to have at their command an extensive repertoire
of linguistic mitigators to express hesitation, to buy time, and
to paraphrase and restate. These skills keep the negotiation
within its prescribed limits, prevent prolonged misunderstandings, and leave the channels of communication open.

When communication breaks down, either for ideological or
for linguistic reasons, students cannot count any longer on the
teacher to do the repair work, check for understanding, give
clues, or use restatement, summary, or paraphrase to redress the
situation. The task of repair is a joint responsibility; it is
a cooperative effort between speakers (Grice 1975). One type of
repair exchange takes the form of "back-channel" activities:
(1) checking of transmission by first speaker ("O.K.?" "Is that
clear, you with me?") followed by go-ahead ("Sure, carry on")
or (2) specification of breakdown by second speaker ("What do
you mean by...?" "I don't see how that ties in with what you
said about..."). As Schwartz (1977) observes, "Repair in conversation is normally the outcome of a negotiation between the
speaker and the listener in order to achieve understanding."

Schwartz' analysis of conversations between adult second
language learners shows that the repair work done by these
learners is similar to repairs done by native speakers. Her
data, collected from three videotaped conversations between
pairs of friends with varying language backgrounds and proficiency levels, show some of the favored "righting mechanisms" by
which speakers help themselves and each other.

If speakers are in trouble or cannot make themselves understood, listeners attempt to locate the trouble source by initi-
ating word searches of their own, "touched off" by the speaker's
speech. They will either partially repeat the turn that is the
source of the trouble, offer a "You mean" and a possible interpretation of the previous turn, or query the entire proposition:

20

"Hm, what?" They might also partially repeat the trouble source and add a question word: "Too many what?"

Speakers themselves will use descriptive gestures or interactive gestures to help themselves or solicit help; with fillers such as "you know," they can fill gaps and stall for time, signalling to their listeners to be patient, indicating to them that the "repaired" expression is coming up right away; or they can use such nonlexical items as "er," "euh," or "ah" as linguistic "space-holders" (Frommer and Ishikawa 1980). Both speakers and listeners work at achieving a "collaborative completion of sentences" and build on each other's speech.

Schwartz concludes that adult second language learners are able and should be given the opportunity to deal with errors and trouble sources and to learn specifics such as vocabulary, as well as conversational strategies, from conversing with one another. She notes that in general, correction in the classroom does not reflect naturally occurring conversation between native speakers. In the classroom, learners' errors are usually corrected--or at least called attention to--even though there is no impairment to hearing or understanding. As a result, many students feel that group work is not useful, because they think they can learn to speak and to converse only from the teacher and not from the other students. In fact, Schwartz' observations show that the fluency of the students is related not only to their proficiency level but also to their interest in each other and to their readiness to negotiate with one another and to struggle for understanding and repair.

If fluency is linked with negotiation for meaning--both self-initiated and other-initiated--we need to re-examine the traditional concept of fluency as it is perceived by and expected of non-native and native speakers of the language. Sajavaara (1978) studied the phenomenon of fluency in non-native and native speakers of English. He found that "it is not the good language competence that is an indicator of fluency, but the perception of the hearer, what sort of attitudes various elements in a speaker's performance trigger in the hearer." By contrasting elements of "perceived fluency" in his subjects, Sajavaara found that the native speakers produced a greater number of false starts, rephrasings, extraneous words, and instances of imprecision and incompletion than non-native speakers, and yet they were perceived to speak more fluently!

Natives did use more subordination of clauses and fewer pauses than the non-native speakers, but instead of pauses they used fillers and other "conversation management devices" necessary to keep the channel open and give them more time to organize their thoughts. As Sajavaara notes, non-natives use more pauses and possibly more repetitions than native speakers because these are the only two ways that they have learned to give themselves more time for finding the correct expression; they have never been taught how else to behave when they have to

keep the communication going but have nothing to say or don't
know how to say what they have to say.

Sajavaara's studies point to the rather paradoxical conclusion that "teaching students how to be disfluent makes them
sound more native-like." For language teachers, aware of the
psychological importance of perceived native-like fluency as a
means of gaining or keeping control of the conversation in the
classroom, the implications of such findings are far-reaching.
Almost all the perceived elements of fluency observed by Sajavaara are of the discursive type; they are interactive tactics
that can be learned and used by the students.

Tables 1b, 2b, 3b (pp. 23-26) summarize some of the strategies that can be taught at the elementary and the more advanced
levels with varying degrees of sophistication. Level one
(beginning students) teaches simple interactional skills; level
two (intermediate and advanced students) deals with more complex
strategies.

The section following Tables 1, 2, and 3 will give some
practical suggestions for discursive activities for the French
and German classrooms. After general activities have been presented that aim at developing the students' readiness to interact, more specific discursive skills can be taught on both the
beginning and the intermediate/advanced levels of proficiency.

Many of these activities are not new, but they are given a
new focus here: (1) they should be viewed and justified within
a discourse analysis framework and not performed as grammatical
exercises; (2) they should be practiced systematically and
integrated into all other activities, not taken as expendable
"conversational gimmicks"; (3) they should be presented to the
students not as exercises in rhetoric but as training in self-
management and autonomous learning.

Table 1

TURN TAKING

A. Description

Natural Discourse Conversational partners' moves, showing readiness to interact	Traditional Classroom Discourse Teacher's moves, showing readiness to teach
Turn Taking (for effective interaction)	Opening (for effective teaching)
1. Find natural completion points	1. Mark boundaries in discourse
2. Take the floor	2. Direct attention
3. Nominate/prime/check/ steer/avoid/change topic	3. Nominate topic, provide information, give clues
4. Select next speaker	4. Nominate responder
5. Give the floor	5. Elicit/demand response
6. Check tactical aspects of interaction	6. Check tactical aspects of lesson

B. Teaching Turn Taking

Level One

Opening/closing conversations
Attracting attention
Interrupting (finding completion points)
Taking the floor (with expression of opinion, assent, or dissent)
Priming topics ("Boston, you know Boston? Well, I live there.")
Identifying topics (finding title, main idea, gist of oral or
    written text)
Checking topic (with paraphrase, question, indirect question)
Predicting questions on topic (brainstorming future course of
    conversation or of reading)
Selecting next speaker (addressing another student)

Level Two

Naming topics ("The thing is...")
Predicting comments and questions ("The question is...")
Priming topics with prefacing markers
Remembering a point and returning to it
Checking and commenting on tactical aspects of interaction
    ("It seems that we all agree...")

23

Table 2

INTERNAL ORGANIZATION OF TURN-AT-TALK

A. Description

Natural Discourse	Traditional Classroom Discourse
Organization within Turn-at-Talk (for successful communication)	Framing and Focusing (for successful progress of lesson)
1. Metacomment and paraphrase	1. Metacomment and paraphrase
2. Expanding through amplification/generalization restriction/contrast examples/examination of causes, consequences, alternatives	2. Expanding through amplification/generalization restriction/contrast examples/examination of causes, consequences, alternatives
3. Internal linking and structuring by announcing future points or by returning to previous points	3. Metastatement and conclusion by structuring future discourse or by summing up past discourse
4. External linking to previous point made by partner	

B. Teaching Paragraph Organization

Level One

Paraphrase with:

Repetition of first element
Repetition of last element
Taxonomic thinking: listing in increasing/decreasing order of
    importance; listing in increasing degree of specificity/
    generality; other organizational principles

Expanding a statement with:

Explanation/clarification ("I mean")
Amplification ("not only this but that")
Restriction ("but")
Contrast ("not this but that")
Examination of causes ("because")
Examination of consequences ("this is why")
Drawing conclusions and making inferences ("so")

Level Two

Expanding a statement with:

Generalization ("on the whole")
Mitigation ("let's say")
Restriction ("however")
Contrasting both sides ("true, yet")
Examining causes, consequences with more elaborate markers
Drawing conclusions and making inferences
Summing up a point

Internal linking and structuring with prefacing markers:

Announcing several points
Prefacing a new point
Making a point (focusing on topic or problem)
Adding a point

External linking to previous speaker's statement by:

Cross-referring, returning to previous point
Adding a point, a comment, a paraphrase, or a counter-argument

Table 3

NEGOTIATION FOR MEANING

A. Description

Natural Discourse	Traditional Classroom Discourse
Negotiation (for proper communication)	Follow-Up and Answering (for proper transmission of material)
1. Accept or request clarification	1. Accept or request clarification
2. Predict, check, match understanding	2. Check understanding
3. Cooperative repair work	3. Evaluate, correct
4. "Back-channel" activities: restatement/repetition, tag question, summarizing, or paraphrase	4. Comment: restatement/ repetition, tag question, summarizing, or paraphrase
5. Buying time, mitigating	

B. Teaching Negotiation for Meaning

Level One

Eliciting clarification (asking to repeat, explain, etc.)
Predict, check, match understanding: systematic brainstorming
   of word associations, circumlocutions, synonyms, antonyms,
   and paraphrases in order to raise level of imagination and
   increase use of contextual knowledge
Repair work: completion of sentences, guessing missing words,
   correct repetition of incorrect sentences
Back-channel activities: reactive listening ("Really?"), partial or total echoing

Level Two

Back-channel activities: voicing opinion, summing up, commenting
Buying time: rephrasing ("so you mean"); paraphrasing ("in
   other words"); hesitating ("well, you know"); mitigating
   ("so to speak"); generalizing ("basically")

26

PRACTICAL APPLICATIONS

Developing Conversational Readiness

Discursive competence cannot be developed independently of other skills. Because it presupposes a general readiness among conversational partners to negotiate, interact, and intervene with one another, preliminary group work is important to stimulate the imagination, reduce self-consciousness, build up confidence and concentration, strengthen belief, and encourage trust and awareness. A first series of games and simulations is aimed at developing conversational readiness. These games raise the level of imagination and aggressiveness of the students, increase their ingenuity and resourcefulness, sharpen their listening skills and their ability to use each other's resources, and make them aware of the importance of the listener. Since the students are encouraged to take risks and to concentrate on "making themselves understood," this is not the time for the teacher to interrupt the activity with remarks on grammar.

The games described below are adaptations for the French and German classrooms of some well known interactional activities in English.[3]

Word Associations

This exercise is frequently used at the elementary level in English classes and is very useful in foreign language classes at all levels to practice the association skills and the piggybacking needed later in conversations. The first student starts with a noun, e.g., das Brot/ le pain (bread), the second student quickly says the first word or group of words he or she associates with the first one, e.g., die Wurst/ le fromage (sausage/cheese), a third student adds, e.g., essen/ manger (to eat), and so on. A variant here is for the player to add a rhythm between the last word and the new word with clapping--twice on the knees, twice in the air, then two silent beats. So we would have: bread--tap, tap; clap, clap; rest, rest; bread, cheese--tap, tap; clap, clap; rest, rest; cheese, eat--tap, tap; clap, clap; rest, rest; etc. This is a good exercise not only for quick thinking and retrieval of vocabulary but also for expanding statements and finding vocabulary alternatives.

What's My Line?

While one student is sent out, the class decides on a word. The student will have to guess that word from associations offered by the other students. At no time should the actual word be used as a cue. For example, the word kochen/ faire la cuisine (to cook) can be guessed from associations such as Abendessen/ dîner (dinner), Frühstück/ petit déjeuner (breakfast), or Feuer/ feu (fire). The student makes suggestions to the group as to which word it could be, and there is quite a bit of negotiating going on between the class and the student to find the right word.

Think Tank

This activity raises the verbal and conceptual imagination of the students and is a good warmup before any class discussion. Students in pairs write down a word such as Wachstum/ croissance (growth) or feige/ peureux (cowardly), or one of the key words in a subsequent discussion topic, e.g., rauchen/ fumer (to smoke), Todesstrafe/ peine capitale (capital punishment) or Werbung/ publicité (publicity). They brainstorm a list of any words or phrases they can associate with that word (explanations, definitions, synonymous or antonymous expressions, or just random associations of ideas). Some pairs of students read out their lists, and other students have to ask questions about the choice of associations.

Brainstorming can also be done by the whole group. The teacher records on the board the ideas suggested, without comment. Students usually build on each other's ideas, and a lively interaction can ensue.

Quarrels

This game raises the level of aggressiveness and the ingenuity of the students as they struggle to build together a fictitious situation. Students work in pairs. The first situation starts with A saying, Nein, das habe ich nicht getan (gesagt)/ Non je n'ai pas fait (dit) ça (No, I didn't)* and B replying, Doch!/ Mais si! (Oh, yes, you did!). This quickly leads into an argument about an obvious cause for disagreement. Students are not allowed to repeat the "No, I didn't/Yes, you did," but must improvise and develop the situation. No time is given for preparation; the players can be given the situation or can imagine it to be anywhere—on a bus, in a shop, in the street, at the breakfast table, or in the classroom. They must start immediately, picking up clues and cues as to who they are imagining that they are in this situation. The exchange is not to last more than one minute, and roles can then be reversed. It need not be a rapid-fire exchange, but each response should build on the previous one as the imagined scenario takes shape.

---

*In this example, as in many others that follow, exact German/ French/English translations are not given. The equivalent words or expressions in each language are provided instead.

Starters

Students work in pairs. Each in turn is given a one-line starter and perhaps the situation for it. The second student must pick up the situation as soon as the first has spoken. By changing the situation, the starter line can be used in various ways:

1. Atmet er noch?/ Est-ce qu'il respire encore? (Is he still breathing?)--on the pavement, in the emergency ward, in the jungle, etc.

2. Tut mir leid, keine Ausländer!/ Pardon, pas d'étrangers! (Sorry, no foreigners!)

3. Warum lässt du dir das Haar nicht schneiden?/ Pourquoi est-ce que tu ne te fais pas couper les cheveux? (Why don't you get your hair cut?)

4. Hat es zwei Köpfe oder sind es drei?/ Ca a deux têtes ou ça en a trois? (Has it got two heads or are there three?)

5. Die sind eine Plage; höchste Zeit, daß man etwas dagegen tut./ C'est une vraie plaie; il est grand temps qu'on fasse quelque chose. (They are a menace; it's time they did something about it.)

6. Jetzt ist's aus; ich hab's zu Hause vergessen./ Ca y est; je l'ai oublié à la maison. (Now we're done for; I forgot to bring it with me.)

7. Wo ist denn mein Holzbein geblieben?/ Où est-ce que j'ai mis ma jambe de bois? (Where on earth has my wooden leg gone?)

Each situation need only be followed for a minute or two, but it gives a good opportunity for the students to activate their imagination and get their cues from one another. The teacher can ask the more imaginative students to re-enact their exchange in front of the whole class.

Waiting Room

This game is to be played in groups of four or five and is a test of ingenuity to keep up differing roles despite a lack of communication. Each player is given a different card on which is stated the reason why he or she is waiting for the dentist, for a train to arrive, for a dog or a cat to be neutered, for a car to be cleaned or repaired, for the result of an interview, or at the gates of heaven. The players must assume that each person is waiting for the same reason as they are. The teacher comes into the room and announces: <u>Es wird nicht mehr lange dauern, nur noch drei Minuten.</u>/ <u>Il n'y en a plus pour très long-temps, plus que trois minutes.</u> (It won't be long now, only three more minutes.)

In a first round, each player has to respond to this opening in turn according to role. He or she then asks questions of the others in their mistaken assumptions. The students must keep a straight face and make comments to the others exclusively from their own point of view without disclosing their reason for being there. Here again a time limit is set (five minutes maximum), after which the students will want to find out what each one was waiting for. In addition to being entertaining, this game makes the students experience the frustration of talking at cross-purposes and the necessity for stepping into someone else's shoes if effective communication is to take place.

The next two games give further practice in this listening skill and understanding of another person's viewpoint.

In Others' Shoes

This game should be played at the beginning of the term, when the students do not yet know each other well. Students are in pairs, A and B. A interviews B in some depth with a time limit of five minutes, asking about background, biography, beliefs, and interests. A then imagines that having interviewed B, he is now actually B, even though each may be of a different sex. For the next three minutes, B interviews "himself," i.e., A. Everything A says must be either what he has been told or what he imagines B would do or say. After the three minutes are up, or after each response, both A and B examine how close some of the invented replies were to the truth or not. The whole exercise can then be reversed with B undertaking the initial interviewing. This game generates a climate of friendship and understanding in the group that is very favorable for subsequent conversations in class.

Broken Roles

This preliminary role-play practices empathy with actions and opinions that are different from what one would expect. In pairs or small groups the following problems are to be solved:

1. Ein Vater (eine Mutter) muß von dem Sohn (der Tochter) Geld borgen./ Un père (une mère) doit emprunter de l'argent à son fils (sa fille). (A father/mother needs to borrow money from a teenage son/daughter.) One student role-plays the father/mother; one or several play the teenager.

30

2. Ein Seekapitän, der seekrank ist/ un capitaine au long
   cours qui a le mal de mer (a sea captain who is sea-
   sick). One student role-plays the captain, and the
   group offers solutions.

3. Ein Richter wird beim Ladendiebstahl erwischt./ Un juge
   est pris en train de voler à l'étalage. (A judge is
   caught shop-lifting.)

4. Ein Arzt beklagt sich immer über seinen Gesundheits-
   zustand./ Un médecin se plaint constamment de son état
   de santé. (A doctor is always complaining that
   something is wrong with him.)

The next series of games will explore our means of communi-
cating by imposing communication handicaps. They make the students aware of all those dimensions of interaction that they
tend to neglect when conversing in the foreign language.

Communication "Minus One"

Facial Expression

A and B sit back-to-back. Heads are not to be twisted
around but must remain looking in opposite directions. Students
arranged in such pairs talk to each other about what they did
over the weekend or describe the arrangement of the furniture in
their room. As when speaking over the phone, the students realize how much easier it is to speak a foreign language when you
can see how the other person reacts to what you say. Hence the
importance of listeners' verbal and nonverbal feedback. Time
limit: three minutes.

Gestures

This time A and B sit facing each other, but they must sit
on their hands while they describe the arrangement of their
rooms, the house of their parents, or an object that the other
student has to guess.
The converse exercise reminds the students of the importance
of nonverbal communication in making yourself understood. A is
given a card with instructions in German or French and has to
convey these instructions to B by mime only. B must guess aloud
what A means to say, by responding or offering a solution. For
example, Frag deinen Partner/ Demande à ton voisin (Ask your
neighbor)

wie spät es ist/ quelle heure il est (what time it is).

ob er/sie Kinder hat/ s'il/si elle a des enfants (if he/she
has any children).

ob er/sie gern schwimmt/ s'il/si elle aime nager (if he/she
likes to swim).

ob er/sie tippen kann/ s'il/si elle sait taper à la machine
(if he/she knows how to type).

ob er/sie Auto fahren kann/ s'il/si elle sait conduire (if
he/she knows how to drive).

ob du mit ihm/ihr zusammenlesen kannst, denn du hast dein
Buch vergessen/ si tu peux suivre sur son livre parce que tu
as oublié le tien (if you can follow in his/her book, for
you have forgotten yours).

These mimes do not require cultural gestures that are specifically German or French; any gestures are good as long as
they convey the desired meaning.

Listener's Feedback

Holding eye contact the whole time, students in pairs are
asked to talk to each other at the same time about a given topic
for a given period--initially 30 seconds, then a minute.
The aim is to keep on talking at all costs and to make the other
person dry up. Players should not be interested in what the
other person is saying but must concentrate on their own story.
A good starting topic is alles was du erlebt hast, seit du heute
morgen aufgewacht bist/ tout ce que tu as fait depuis que tu
t'es levé ce matin (everything that happened to you from the
time you woke up this morning). Other suggestions are: deine
Lieblingsgeschichte/ ton histoire préférée (your favorite story)
or du mußt unbedingt dein Fahrrad verkaufen/ il faut absolument
que tu vendes ton vélo (you absolutely have to sell your bicy-
cle). The topic should be an easy one that can be done immediately off the top of the students' heads with vocabulary they
already know. This is an excellent starter. It makes a lot of
noise and generates much laughter. Neither player hears the
other; there is no interaction, no dialogue, no relationship.
This game challenges students to outspeak their partners, to be
aggressive, to keep the floor at all costs. The teacher points
out after the game the difficulty of having an exchange when the
listener does not respond or acknowledge listening in any way.
These preliminary exercises can provide the behavioral
framework and the spirit for future student-student interaction
in the classroom. They are warmup activities that set the tone
for active listening and spontaneous reacting, for aggressiveness in turn taking and keeping the floor, and for inventiveness

32

in thought and speech. Five or ten minutes spent on one or two
such exercises are quite enough for a given period. The class
needs to understand the relevance of the warmup before it pro-
ceeds to more skill-oriented activities.

Learning Conversational Management

From observing how native speakers manage their discourse,
students can learn how to use the foreign language in the same
manner. Tape recorded conversations, discussions, and interviews in authentic situations should be given to the students to
listen to. These may be the same tapes that are generally used
for the retrieval of cultural or lexical information, but here
the aim is to identify the characteristic discursive features of
speech. Inter Nationes offers much authentic material in German
suitable for this purpose and so do the series of French tapes
published by the Bureau pour l'Enseignement de la Langue et de
la Civilisation Française à l'Etranger or by the Harvard Modern
Language Center.4

Selected passages are carefully transcribed with pauses,
hesitations, redundancies, etc., and given to the students to
analyze. Next, the individual features of discourse are isolated and discussed. They are then practiced in combination in
a simulated situation or in a class discussion. A sample of
this three-step approach is given for French and German in
Appendix 1.

The following exercises are suggestions for practicing some
of the individual discursive skills: (1) taking the floor and
directing the topic, (2) keeping the floor and linking, (3) back-
channel activities. The two other most important skills--buying
time and mitigating--are essential to all three categories.
These sample exercises can be expanded and varied according to
the needs and level of the class. Some of them involve using
verbal cues to fulfill specific discursive functions. A list of
some of the major linguistic cues in French and German can be
found in Appendix 2.

Taking the Floor (Turn Taking)

Interrupting the teacher. This is a whole-group activity. The
teacher starts to talk on any chosen topic. Students have five
or ten minutes--according to the size of the class--to interrupt, using one of the attention getters listed in Appendix 2,
numbers 1.1-1.4. Every student must interrupt the teacher at
least once, if ever so briefly, and the interruption must be
followed by a comment/question/remark. The teacher responds
briefly to the comment and returns to the topic with one of the
links listed under no. 12. The teacher then goes on talking
until the next interruption.

Interrupting the class. Students choose their favorite attention getter and have to use it during normal class activities to
interrupt the teacher or a fellow student before the end of the
period. The challenge is to have the interruption occur in the
natural context of the classroom and to identify an appropriate
moment to interrupt. The person interrupted has to respond to
the interruption and then use a link to return to the topic.
Students score one point for using their interrupter appropriately and successfully.

This exercise is not as easy as it looks, for it involves
careful listening to find the right moment to make an appropriate comment. But the students like the sense of power that
comes from being able to manage classroom discourse.

Interrupting a fellow student. This exercise can be added to
any activity that requires groups of four or five students to
get together to brainstorm an issue, make a list of word associations, discuss the content of a reading, or prepare a skit.
Two or three students go from group to group, listen in for a
while, and then interrupt the speaker with a polite or aggressive attention getter followed by a remark. Speakers have to
acknowledge the interruption and use a link to return to their
topic. Some of the expressions listed under no. 11 will be
needed if the interrupter becomes too aggressive.

Opinion opening. The teacher lists a choice of opinion openers
(2.1-2.4) and responders (17-22) on the board, of a difficulty
level appropriate for the group. Students in groups of three
are shown different inkblots. In turn they have to say what
they see in these inkblots, using one of the opinion openers.
The next student has to respond with a cue asking for clarification or showing surprise, assent, or dissent. Then he or she
expresses an opinion about the inkblot, using a hesitation or an
opinion opener.

Dear Abby. Students in groups of five are given a "problem" to
solve. One student reads aloud the problem, and each of the
other four students makes a personal suggestion starting with
Ich finde, du könntest/ Je trouve que tu pourrais (I think you
could), or Ich meine, du solltest/ Je pense que tu devrais (I
think you should), or An deiner Stelle würde ich/ Si j'étais
toi, je (If I were you). The student rejects one suggestion
after another for reasons that must be stated. Then another
student reads aloud another problem and the group once again
offers suggestions. Some examples:

1. Ich habe einen tollen Gebrauchtwagen gefunden. Der
    Besitzer fährt morgen nach Mexico und will nur 1500 DM
    dafür haben. Aber er muß das Geld bar haben. Was soll
    ich tun?/ Je viens de trouver une voiture d'occasion

sensationnelle. Le propriétaire doit partir demain pour le Mexique et ne demande que 3000 FF, mais il les veut en liquide. Qu'est-ce que je dois faire? (I've found a great second-hand car. The owner is going to Mexico tomorrow and is asking only $700 for it, but he wants cash. What should I do?)

2. Ich habe aus Versehen meine Schlüssel im Wagen gelassen und den Wagen abgeschlossen. Was soll ich tun?/ J'ai enfermé mes clefs dans la voiture par mégarde. Qu'est-ce que je dois faire? (I've locked my car keys in the car by mistake. What should I do?)

3. Meine Katze hat alle ihre Haare verloren. Was soll ich tun?/ Mon chat a perdu tous ses poils. Qu'est-ce que je dois faire? (My cat has lost all its hair. What should I do?)

4. Jeden Morgen, wenn ich den Wecker abgeschaltet habe, schlafe ich wieder ein und komme spät in die Klasse. Was soll ich tun?/ Tous les matins quand j'ai arrêté mon réveil, je me rendors et je suis en retard pour mes cours. Qu'est-ce que je dois faire? (Every morning after turning off my alarm clock, I go back to sleep and am late for class. What should I do?)

Students are then given two minutes to think up their own problem. Student A starts with Ich habe ein Problem/ J'ai un problème (I have a problem), and each student has to come up with one suggestion starting with an opinion opener.

Press conference. The teacher brainstorms and lists on the board students' suggestions for topics on which there may be divergent opinions, such as Deutsch lernen/ apprendre le français (learn French/German), Diskomusik/ la musique disco (disco music), klassische Musik/ la musique classique (classical music), MacDonald's, etc. Or the teacher may suggest some outrageous topic such as Brauchen Studenten überhaupt Schlaf?/ Est-ce qu'un étudiant a besoin de sommeil? (Do students need sleep at all?), Sollte der Lehrer den Studenten vor der Prüfung ein Glas Bier geben?/ Devrait-on donner aux étudiants un verre de vin avant l'examen? (Should students be given a glass of beer/wine before exams?), Sollten Studenten ein Gehalt bekommen?/ Un étudiant devrait-il recevoir un salaire? (Should students be paid a salary for studying?), or Sollte Karate an der Oberschule Pflichtfach sein?/ Devrait-on enseigner le karate à l'école comme sujet obligatoire? (Should karate be a required course in high school?).

In both variations students are given one minute to form an opinion. The exercise is run like the "Opinion Opening" exer-

cise, but with the whole class. It should be made clear that
they don't have to voice their personal opinion about the matter; far-out opinions and totally unrealistic viewpoints are
encouraged.

Current affairs. The same exercise can be prepared as written
homework on more complex issues and with more formal opinion
openers as groundwork for a debate. Students are asked to list
three arguments for and three arguments against the following
topics:

1. Entwicklungshilfe/ aide aux pays en voie de développe-
   ment (aid to developing countries)

2. Trinkalter: 20 Jahre/ alcool interdit aux moins de 20
   ans (drinking age: 20)

3. die Todesstrafe/ le peine capitale (capital punishment)

4. das Automobil/ l'automobile (the automobile)

5. die Olympischen Spiele/ les jeux olympiques (Olympic
   games)

6. das Telefon/ le téléphone (the telephone)

In pairs, students have to preface their arguments with an
opinion marker and respond to their partner's argument with a
cue giving acknowledgment and feedback.

Focus on the main thing. The teacher brainstorms the group as
to where their priorities lie: Was ist für dich das Wichtigste/
Quelle est pour toi la chose la plus importante (What is the
most important thing for you)

wenn du ein College wählst?/ quand tu choisis un collège?
(when you choose a college?)

wenn du einen Kurs belegst?/ quand tu choisis un cours?
(when you choose a course?)

wenn du einen Job suchst?/ quand tu cherches un job? (when
you look for a job?)

wenn du einen Freund/eine Freundin suchst?/ quand tu
cherches un(e) ami(e)? (when you look for a friend?)

wenn du ein Zimmer suchst?/ quand tu cherches une chambre?
(when you are looking for a room?)

Each student should answer with one of the following openers:

Die Hauptsache für mich ist:*
Für mich geht es nur um eins:
Es kommt für mich darauf an, daß...(verb)

Pour moi, l'essentiel c'est que (+ subjunctive)
La chose la plus importante pour moi c'est
Ce qui est important, c'est de savoir

(The main thing for me is/ The most important thing for me
is/ I am mainly concerned about)

<u>Focus on the main problem.</u> The teacher brainstorms the group as
to where the students perceive the main difficulty to be: <u>Was
ist für dich die Hauptfrage/ Quel est pour toi le problème prin-
cipal</u> (What is the main problem, as far you are concerned)

beim Heiraten?/ quand on veut se marier? (when you get
married?)

beim Fremdsprachenlernen?/ quand on apprend une langue
étrangère? (when you learn a foreign language?)

wenn man einen Hund hat?/ quand on a un chien? (when you
have a dog?)

wenn man zuviel fernsieht?/ quand on passe son temps devant
la télé? (when you watch too much TV?)

The students answer with one of the following openers:

Die Frage ist die:
Die eigentliche Frage ist nämlich, daß...(verb)
Es geht nur um die Frage:

Le problème c'est que (+ indicative)/c'est de (+ infinitive)
Au fond c'est une question de
Il faut d'abord savoir si

(The problem is/ It is mainly a question of/ The main
question is)

---

*The position of the predicate in the statements that follow the
German openers is as follows: at the end of the dependent
clause if introduced by <u>daß</u>, in second position (as in a main
clause) if introduced by a colon.

Redirecting the topic. As a whole class or in small groups, students have to redirect the topic as they wish from cues taken from another student's statement, using the digression markers listed in Appendix 2, no. 4. Students are to make around each of the following cues one or two sentences or as many as needed before another student interrupts: Letztes Wochenende--tolle Party--Neujahr/ Le week-end dernier--une soirée formidable--le Nouvel An (last weekend--great party--New Year). The student who interrupted then continues with a different sequence of associations.

Example: A: Ich habe letztes Wochenende zwölf Stunden
              geschlafen; das war herrlich--
           B: Wenn du schon vom Wochenende redest, da war ich
              Samstag bei einer tollen Party; es gab so viel zu
              essen!--
           C: A propos Party: da kann ich mich noch an unsere
              Neujahrsparty erinnern.

           A: Le week-end dernier j'ai dormi douze heures,
              c'était formidable--
           B: Parlant de week-end, je suis allé samedi à une
              soirée sensationnelle; il y avait tellement à
              manger!--
           C: A propos de soirée, je me souviens encore de cette
              soirée du Nouvel An.

(Last weekend I slept 12 hours, it was great--Speaking of weekends, I went to a fantastic party Saturday; there was so much food!--By the way, I still remember that New Year's party.)

A conversation may move too quickly beyond the point where a participant wishes to intervene. Remembering a point one wishes to return to or refer to and then linking up with that point is one of the most difficult things to do in a foreign language. It should be practiced and encouraged systematically in the course of the normal classroom activities and within the exercises to interrupt the teacher.

Keeping the Floor (Internal Organization
of the Turn-at-Talk)

Paraphrase for greater specificity. Students should systematically practice paraphrasing as early as the beginning levels, for it is one of the major elements of fluency and conversational "punch." They can use simple or more sophisticated vocabulary according to their level.
   This can be an individual written exercise or a brainstorming of the whole group in class. The latter has the advantage

tage of enabling the students to build on each other's ideas.
Students can also work in small groups and see which group comes
up with the longest list of paraphrases.

Explain with paraphrases the underlined element in the following
statements, going from the general to the particular.

Example with colon (no connector):

Man sieht viel Gewalttätigkeit [general] im Fernsehen:
man sieht viel Blut, man sieht viele Tote, die Polizei
schießt, Verbrecher schießen [particular].

On voit beaucoup de violence [general] à la télé: on
voit du sang, on voit des morts, la police tire sur les
gens, les gens tirent sur la police [particular].

(There is a lot of violence [general] on TV: a lot of
bloodshed, a lot of killing going on, a lot of shooting
by the police and by the criminals [particular].)

Example with connector (German-specific):

Ich reise gern, und zwar fahre ich gern nach dem Süden,
nach Florida, ich fahre auch gern nach Europa.

(I like to travel, that is, I like to travel to the
South, to Florida; I also like to travel to Europe.)

1. Im Moment lerne ich viel, (und zwar)/ En ce moment
    j'apprends beaucoup de choses: (Right now, I am learning
    a lot:)

2. In Amerika kann jeder tun was er will, (nämlich),/ En
    Amérique chacun peut faire ce qu'il veut: (In America,
    everyone can do what he likes:)

3. In Amerika kann man die Kinder überall mitnehmen,
    (nämlich)/ En Amérique on peut emmener ses enfants
    partout: (In America you can take the children along
    with you anywhere:)

4. Mein Freund ist sehr hilfsbereit, (nämlich)/ Mon copain
    est toujours prêt à rendre service: (My friend is
    always very helpful:)

5. Das Studentenleben bietet viele Vorteile, (und zwar):/
    la vie d'étudiant a beaucoup d'avantages: (There are
    many advantages to being a student:)

Paraphrase with synonymous statements. Rather than the more
traditional search for synonyms, this is a brainstorming of all
the possible ways to express roughly the same meaning. Student
A has to explain to student B, who has only a basic knowledge of
the foreign language, what he means. He offers him or her two
or three equivalent statements.

Example: A: Ich bin einfach überarbeitet.
           B: Wie meinst du das?
           A: Na ja, ich habe zuviel Arbeit, ich habe keine Zeit
              zu schlafen, ich bin sehr müde, ich gehe bald
              kaputt.
           B: Ach so!

           A: Je suis complètement surmené.
           B: Qu'est-ce que tu veux dire?
           A: Eh bien, j'ai trop de travail, je manque de
              sommeil, je suis crevé, quoi!
           B: Ah bon!

(I am simply overworked. What do you mean? Well, I just
have too much to do, I get too little sleep, I am tired,
dead beat. Ah ha!)

On the same model of dialogue, pairs of students are to paraphrase the following:

1. Ich kümmere mich nicht um Zensuren./ Les notes, je ne
    m'en soucie pas. (I don't care about grades.)

2. Das Telefon ist eine Plage./ Le téléphone est une plaie.
    (The telephone is a nuisance.)

3. Regenschirme sind gefährlich./ Les parapluies sont
    dangereux. (Umbrellas are dangerous.)

4. Die Institution der Ehe ist schädlich./ Le mariage est
    nuisible. (Marriage is harmful.)

5. Alte Leute gehören ins Altersheim./ Les vieillards à
    l'asile de vieillards. (Old folks should be in old
    folks' homes.)

With the use of the paraphrase, speakers not only make themselves more explicit, but they manage to hold the floor for as
long as they have something more to say or to add.

Expand for greater generality. Going around the room, the
teacher elicits expansions on a given statement. Three or four
students repeat the initial statement, and each builds upon it

by adding a new variation of the underlined elements; a fifth student draws a general conclusion using the cue überhaupt/ enfin, bref, or quoi.

Example: A: Ich mag nicht unpünktlich sein, wenn ich eine Verabredung habe.
           B: Ich mag nicht unpünktlich sein, wenn ich ins Kino gehe.
           C: Ich mag nicht unpünktlich sein, wenn ich in die Schule gehe.
           D: Ich mag nicht unpünktlich sein, wenn ich eingeladen bin.
           E: Ich bin überhaupt ein sehr pünktlicher Mensch.

           A: Je n'aime pas arriver en retard à un rendez-vous.
           B: Je n'aime pas arriver en retard au cinéma.
           C: Je n'aime pas arriver en retard à l'école.
           D: Je n'aime pas arriver en retard quand je suis invité(e).
           E: Bref (enfin), j'aime toujours être à l'heure (quoi).

(I don't like to be late when I have an appointment; I don't like to be late when I go to the movies; I don't like to be late when I go to school; I don't like to be late when I am invited somewhere; [in fact] I am a very punctual person.)

Following the example above, expand each of the following sentences with three or four variations of the underlined elements, then sum up with a generalizing statement.

1. Ich habe keine Zeit, die Zeitung zu lesen; ich habe keine Zeit/ Je n'ai pas le temps de lire le journal; je n'ai pas le temps de (I don't have time to read the newspaper; I don't have time to)

2. Mein Hund frißt Brot; er frißt/ Mon chien mange du pain; il mange (My dog eats bread; he eats)

3. Ich mag keine Katzen; ich mag keine/ Je n'aime pas les chats; je n'aime pas (I don't like cats; I don't like)

4. Mit 20 Jahren darf man trinken; man darf/ A 20 ans on a le droit de boire; on a le droit de (At 20 you are allowed to drink; you are allowed to)

5. Im Urlaub möchte man nicht an die Lehrer denken; man möchte nicht/ En vacances on veut oublier les professeurs; on veut oublier (On vacation you don't want to think of your teachers; you don't want to think of)

At a second stage, all four or five paraphrases can be provided by the same student, as native speakers do when they want to expand their turn at talk.

Restricting. The class is divided into pessimists and optimists. The optimists have to find the good side of each statement the pessimists make, starting with any of the cues listed under 6.6 in Appendix 2.

1. Das Essen in der Mensa ist miserabel!/ La nourriture à la cantine est infecte! (The food in the cafeteria is awful!)

2. Mein Job ist langweilig!/ Mon travail est d'un ennuyeux! (My job is so boring!)

3. Meine Freundin geht mit einem anderen./ Mon amie sort avec un autre. (My friend is dating someone else.)

4. Meine Miete ist zu hoch./ Mon loyer est trop cher. (My rent is too high.)

5. Diskomusik ist eintönig!/ La musique disco est monotone! (Disco music is monotonous!)

Now it is up to the pessimists to tone down the enthusiasm of the optimists by showing them the other side of the coin, using allerdings/évidemment (of course).

Example: Ich habe eine tolle Wohnung!--Allerdings ist sie ein bißchen teuer./ J'ai un appartement sensationnel!-- Evidemment il est un peu cher. (I have a great apartment!--Of course, it is a little expensive.)

1. Ich habe die ganze Wohnung saubergemacht!/ J'ai nettoyé tout l'appartement! (I cleaned the whole apartment!)

2. Ich habe 5 Pfund abgenommen!/ J'ai perdu 3 kilos! (I lost 5 pounds!)

3. Ich habe gestern einen tollen Film gesehen!/ J'ai vu hier un film sensationnel! (I saw a great movie yesterday!)

4. Ich habe eine Reise nach Deutschland gewonnen!/ Je viens de gagner un voyage en France! (I just won a trip to Germany/France!)

5. Meine Freunde kommen morgen zu Besuch!/ Mes copains

viennent me voir demain! (My friends are coming
tomorrow for a visit!)

Contrasting both sides. Speakers can use contrast strategies to
expand a point. Students are given three minutes to think of
two sides for the following issues. They are to express both
sides using the cues listed under 6.7 in Appendix 2.

Example: In Boston wohnen?--Einerseits ist die Stadt schön und
         alt, andererseits ist der Winter dort wirklich sehr
         kalt./ Vivre à Boston?--Hm. D'un côté la ville est
         belle et relativement ancienne, d'un autre côté,
         l'hiver y est vraiment très froid. (Live in Boston?
         --Hm. On the one hand it's a beautiful old city, on
         the other hand, the winters are terribly cold.)

   1. Trinkalter: 20 Jahre/ l'alcool interdit aux moins de 20
       ans (drinking age: 20)

   2. Zoos/ les zoos

   3. Zensuren/ les notes (grades)

   4. Studentinnenheime/ maisons pour étudiantes seulement
       (women's dorms)

   5. Frauen beim Militär/ service militaire pour les femmes
       (military service for women)

More contrasting. To predispose the listener favorably to
something you have to say, it is a good tactic to acknowledge
first what that listener has said earlier. To contrast one
point with a point previously made, Germans use the double link
zwar...aber; the French use il est vrai que...mais n'empêche que
(+ indicative).

Example: Du hast zwar eine schöne Wohnung, aber sie ist
         unwahrscheinlich teuer!/ Il est vrai que tu as un bel
         appartement, mais n'empêche qu'il est rudement cher!
         (True, you have a nice apartment, but it is terribly
         expensive!)

Student A offers a statement that student B counters with the
appropriate cues.

Prejudices and truths. You may contrast in this manner what
people think and what is actually true.

Example: Viele Leute glauben zwar, daß Columbus Amerika ent-
         deckt hat, aber in Wirklichkeit war es Leif Ericson./

43

Beaucoup de gens pensent que c'est Christophe Colomb qui a découvert l'Amérique, <u>or</u> <u>en</u> <u>fait</u> c'est Leif Ericson. (Many people believe that Christopher Columbus discovered America, but in fact it was Leif Ericson.)

In the same way, point out the flaw in the following catch phrases:

1. Man fährt schneller mit dem Flugzeug./ On voyage beaucoup plus vite en avion. (You can travel faster by plane.)

2. Butter ist gut gegen Brandwunden./ Le beurre est bon pour les brûlures. (Butter is good for burns.)

3. Französisch ist eine leichte Sprache./ Le français est une langue facile. (French is an easy language.)

4. Männer sind stärker als Frauen./ Les hommes sont plus forts que les femmes. (Men are stronger than women.)

5. Studenten führen das schönste Leben./ Les étudiants ont la belle vie. (Students have the best life.)

Offer your own stereotyped statement and have another student counter it.

<u>Appearance and reality</u>. You may contrast appearances and reality with the same cues.

Example: Es sieht <u>zwar</u> so aus, als ob es ein Schmetterling wäre, <u>aber</u> <u>in</u> <u>Wirklichkeit</u> ist es ein Tintenfleck./ On dirait que c'est un papillon, <u>mais</u> <u>en</u> <u>réalité</u> c'est une tache d'encre. (It may look like a butterfly, but it's really an inkspot.)

In the same way, contrast the following:

1. meine Schwester--meine Mutter/ ma soeur--ma mère (my sister--my mother)

2. Wasser--Schnaps/ eau--eau-de-vie (water--gin)

3. Rotwein--Essig/ vin rouge--vinaigre (red wine--vinegar)

4. echte Blumen--Plastikblumen/ vraies fleurs--fleurs en plastique (real flowers--plastic flowers)

5. ein netter Mensch--?/ une personne sympathique--? (a nice person--?)

Suggest one "appearance" yourself, and another student will provide the "reality."

Finding excuses. Using one of the cues listed in 6.8, find a plausible justification in response to the following accusations:

1. Du hast nicht auf meinen Brief geantwortet!/ Tu n'as pas répondu à ma lettre! (You didn't answer my letter!)

2. Du hast mir mein Buch immer noch nicht zurückgegeben!/ Tu ne m'as toujours pas rendu mon livre! (You still haven't returned my book!)

3. Du hast mich nicht angerufen, wie du versprochen hattest!/ Tu ne m'as pas téléphoné, comme tu me l'avais promis! (You didn't call as you promised!)

4. Du hast den Müll nicht hinausgetragen!/ Tu n'as pas sorti les ordures! (You didn't take out the garbage!)

5. Du bist spät in die Klasse gekommen!/ Tu es arrivé en classe en retard! (You were late for class!)

Getting out of a tight spot. Often in a job interview, you have to explain why you did certain things or why something happened. The more embarrassing the question, the more you will want to use mitigators and longer discursive devices.

1. Sie haben während des Schuljahres 25 Stunden pro Woche gearbeitet. Warum?/ Je vois que vous avez travaillé 25 heures par semaine pendant l'année scolaire. Pourquoi? (You worked 25 hours a week during the school year. Why?)

2. Sie sind nur sechs Monate bei Ihrer letzten Stelle geblieben. Warum?/ Vous n'êtes resté que six mois dans votre dernier emploi. Pourquoi? (You only stayed six months in your last job. Why?)

3. Sie haben noch nicht nach dem Gehalt gefragt. Warum?/ Vous ne m'avez pas encore demandé quel serait le salaire. Pourquoi? (You haven't asked yet about the salary. Why not?)

Students in pairs simulate employer and prospective employee in such a situation.

<u>Examining causes</u>. In a discussion, examining causes is a very useful strategy to strengthen a point. Expand the following statements, using some of the longer causality markers under no. 6.8.

1. Viele Schüler haben noch Angst vor ihrem Lehrer./ Bien des élèves ont encore peur de leur professeur. (Many students are still afraid of their teacher.)

2. In vielen Berufen wird immer noch gegen Frauen diskriminiert./ Dans bien des professions il y a encore de la discrimination contre les femmes. (In many professions, women are still discriminated against.)

3. Fernsehwerbung ist sehr teuer./ La publicité à la télé coûte très cher. (Publicity on TV is very expensive.)

4. Viele Länder der Welt sind überbevölkert./ Beaucoup de pays sont surpeuplés. (Many countries in the world are overpopulated.)

<u>Announcing several points</u>. By using cues listed under no. 7, the speaker can capture the attention of the listener for as long as needed to make a second point. Here is a telephone conversation explaining why you won't be able to do what your friend suggests. Announce the number of reasons with <u>Aus</u> <u>X</u> <u>Gründen</u>/ <u>Pour</u> <u>X</u> <u>raisons</u> (For X reasons), then preface your first reason by <u>erstens</u>, <u>zuerst</u> <u>mal</u>, or <u>nicht</u> <u>nur</u>/ d'<u>abord</u>, <u>la</u> <u>première</u> <u>c'est</u> <u>que</u>, or <u>non</u> <u>seulement</u> (first, the first is, not only) and your subsequent reasons by <u>und</u> <u>dann</u>, <u>zweitens</u> or <u>sondern</u> <u>auch</u>/ <u>ensuite</u>, <u>deuxième</u><u>ment</u> or <u>mais</u> <u>aussi</u> (then, second, but also).

1. Warum lernst du nicht Russisch?/ Pourquoi est-ce que tu n'apprends pas le russe? (Why don't you learn Russian?)

2. Warum fährst du diesen Sommer nicht nach Deutschland?/ Pourquoi est-ce que tu ne vas pas en France cet été? (Why don't you go to Germany/France this summer?)

3. Warum läßt du dir das Haar nicht schneiden?/ Pourquoi ne te fais-tu pas couper les cheveux? (Why don't you get a haircut?)

Here are some questions that children love to ask. Adults generally invent reasons and cover up their embarrassment with serious sounding cues. Find some.

1. Warum hat die Giraffe einen so langen Hals?/ Pourquoi est-ce que la girafe a un si long cou? (Why does the giraffe have such a long neck?)

2. Warum ist die Banane krumm?/ Pourquoi est-ce que le melon a des tranches? (Why are bananas curved? Why do melons come with slices?)

3. Warum ist die Suppe immer so heiß?/ Pourquoi est-ce que la soupe est toujours si chaude? (Why is soup always so hot?)

Adding a point. To keep from being interrupted once you have made a point, you may want to announce your next point with one of the cues listed under no. 8. Using first Der Grund, warum ...ist daß/ La raison pour laquelle...est que (The reason why... is that), then going on to Hinzu kommt noch, daß/ Il faut dire aussi que (In addition), answer the following questions:

1. Warum rauchst du nicht mehr?/ Tu ne fumes plus? (Why have you stopped smoking?)

2. Warum brauchst du 1 000 Dollar?/ Pourquoi est-ce que tu as besoin de 1 000 dollars? (Why do you need 1,000 dollars?)

3. Warum sollte ich Chinesisch lernen?/ Pourquoi apprendre le chinois? (Why should I learn Chinese?)

4. Warum sollte Sexualkunde in der Schule unterrichtet werden?/ Pourquoi est-ce qu'on devrait enseigner l'éducation sexuelle à l'école? (Why should sex education be taught in the schools?)

Linking by restating. To "keep the ball rolling," speakers use a statement made by another speaker as a starting point for their own. For this you have to know how to repeat what you have just heard, reformulate it, and/or summarize it. As a whole-class activity, the teacher asks simple questions of the students, who have to repeat the question in indirect discourse and then give an answer (as people do when they want to make quite sure that they have heard properly and that they understand the topic).

Example: Wie heißt du?--Wie ich heiße? Peter.
Gehst du bald nach Hause?--Ob ich bald nach Hause gehe? Ja, in fünf Minuten.
Was hältest du von deinen Kursen?--Was ich davon halte? Na ja....

Comment est-ce que tu t'appelles?--Comment je m'appelle? Pierre.
Est-ce que tu vas bientôt rentrer?--Si je vais bientôt rentrer? Ben oui, dans cinq minutes.

> Que penses-tu de tes cours?--Ce que j'en pense? Ben,
> tu sais....

(What's your name?--My name? Peter. Are you going home
soon?--Me? Going home? Yeah, in five minutes. What do you
think of your classes?--What I think of them? Well,....)

The students may be asked to repeat only part of the question
before they answer.

Example: Gehst du bald nach Hause?--Bald? Nein, erst in zwei
          Stunden.
          Was hältst du vom Wetter hier in Boston?--Vom Wetter?
          Was ich davon halte? Nun,....

          Tu vas bientôt rentrer?--Bientôt, non, seulement dans
          deux heures.
          Que penses-tu du temps ici à Boston?--Le temps? Ce
          que j'en pense? Ben....

(Are you going home soon?--Soon? Me? Going home? What do
you think of the weather here in Boston?--The weather? In
Boston? Well,....)

Students then break into pairs. Student A expresses an opinion
about an issue and keeps on talking until student B interrupts
and checks his or her understanding of A's opinion by repeating
it or by summarizing or reformulating it (see no. 13). A
accepts or does not accept B's interpretation of what he or she
said.

Example: Die Rolle der Polizei

   A: Ich finde, die Polizei sollte eine größere Rolle
       spielen, sie sollte die Straßen mehr patrouillieren, da
       hätten wir weniger Kriminalität.

   B: Du meinst, die Polizei sollte mehr Schutz bieten?

   A: Ja genau!

Example: Le rôle de la police

   A: Je trouve que la police devrait jouer un rôle plus
       actif, devrait patrouiller plus souvent les rues, on
       aurait moins de criminalité.

   B: Donc d'après toi, la police devrait offrir plus de
       sécurité?

   A: C'est ça.

(The role of the police. A: I feel the police should be more active, they should patrol the streets more often, we would have less crime. B: You mean the police should offer more protection? A: Right!)

Use the same linking devices for such issues as Zensuren/ les notes (grades); Haustiere/ les animaux domestiques (pets); Hausaufgaben/ les devoirs (homework), etc.

Cross-referring. The conversation often rolls along so quickly that you never have a chance to say what you wanted to say. You need to practice returning to a previous point (see "Redirecting the Topic," p. 38). The teacher talks uninterruptedly for two minutes. Students should not interrupt but instead note which word or phrase they want to get back to when the teacher stops talking. Each student in turn then takes the floor with the appropriate cue (no. 14) followed by a comment or a question.

Counter-argument. In a German or a French discussion, you should not hesitate to interrupt at any point, as soon as you feel you have a valid counter-argument. In the following game, students play the role of salespeople. They decide which product they want to sell and prepare a one-line ad and a series of persuasive arguments. Working in pairs, Student A makes a sales pitch; Student B counters every argument with one of the cues under no. 16.1 or 16.2. The challenge is for the salesperson to hold on as long as possible without repeating anything. Then roles are reversed, and the B's make their sales pitch.

Example: Lernen Sie fließend Deutsch sprechen in 10 Stunden!
            Parlez couramment le français en dix leçons!
            (Learn to speak fluent German/French in 10 lessons!)

            Neuer Merzedes für nur 300 Dollar!
            Citroën neuve pour 300 dollars!
            (A new Mercedes/Citroën for only 300 dollars!)

            Baby-sitting: nur 10 cents die Stunde!
            Baby-sitting: à dix cents de l'heure!
            (Baby-sitting for only 10 cents an hour!)

Back-Channel Activities (Negotiating for Meaning)

Asking for clarification. This exercise offers practice in interrupting on the spot if something is unclear. It simulates the difficulties encountered by receptionists on the telephone trying to get accurate information. Telephone receptionists on emergency posts typically use cues such as those listed under no. 17: Wie bitte? Was meinen Sie? Verzeihung, wie war das?

49

Wie war das noch mal? Ich habe das nicht mitgekriegt, können
Sie das wiederholen?/ Pardon? Comment? Qu'est-ce que vous
dites? Pardon, vous dites? Vous voulez répéter? (Excuse me?
What did you say? Sorry, what was that? What was that again?
I didn't catch that, could you repeat that please?)

Practice an emergency call with another student in the
class. You, Student B, are the telephone receptionist and
should try to get the information indicated below. The caller,
Student A, might be upset because of the emergency of the situation, so be patient and understanding as well as efficient. Both
students receive cards with instructions. Some examples:

1. Notruf bei der Feuerwehr

   A: Hier ist Notzustand in der Prinz-Ferdinandstraße, Nummer
      86. Ein Feuer ist im 6. Stockwerk eines großen Wohn-
      hauses ausgebrochen. Dicker schwarzer Rauch strömt aus
      den Fenstern der Wohnung, füllt den Flur und einen Teil
      des Treppenhauses.

   B: Notieren Sie sich die genaue Adresse und Nummer des
      Hauses und der Wohnung, Beschreibung des Gebäudes, Name
      und Adresse des Anrufenden. Sagen Sie ihm, er solle den
      Feueralarm geben und die Treppe benutzen, nicht den Auf-
      zug. Die Feuerwehr komme bald.

2. Urgence chez les pompiers

   A: Urgence chez les pompiers. Un incendie s'est déclaré au
      numéro 35 rue Charles-Lafitte dans un appartement du 5e
      étage. Une épaisse fumée noire sort des fenêtres et
      remplit déjà la cage d'escalier.

   B: Notez l'adresse exacte de l'incendie, description de
      l'immeuble, nom et adresse de la personne au téléphone.
      Dites-lui de tirer l'alarme et de ne pas utiliser
      l'ascenseur pour descendre mais de prendre l'escalier.
      Les pompiers seront là dans quelques minutes.

(Emergency call at the fire station. A: This is an
emergency. There is a fire on the Xth floor of a large
apartment building at such and such an address. Heavy black
smoke is pouring out of the windows of the apartment and is
filling the hallways and part of the stairwell. B: Note
down exact address, house and apartment number, type of
building, name and address of caller. Tell him to call the
fire alarm and to use the stairs, not the elevator. Tell
him the fire trucks will be there soon.)

3. Notruf bei der Polizei

   A: Es hat einen Streit gegeben zwischen einem großen dicken
      Griechen und einem etwas dünneren Italiener in der Nach-

50

barkneipe. Es hat Messerstiche gegeben und der Grieche
blutet am Kopf.

B: Notieren Sie sich Adresse der Kneipe, Beschreibung der
Streitenden, Name und Adresse des Anrufenden. Sagen Sie
ihm, der Polizeiwagen sei unterwegs.

4. <u>Urgence au commissariat de police</u>

A: Une bagarre a éclaté au bistro entre un Grec et un Ita-
lien. Quelq'un a tiré un couteau et le Grec est blessé
à la tête.

B: Notez l'adresse exacte du bistro, description des participants dans la bagarre, nom et adresse de la personne
au téléphone. Dites-lui que la police sera là dans
quelques minutes.

(Emergency call at the police station. A: There has been a
fight in the bar next door between a Greek and an Italian.
They've drawn knives and the Greek is bleeding from the
head. B: Get the address of the bar and the description of
the men who are fighting, the name and address of the
caller. Tell him that a police car is on the way.)

5. Your own emergency.

<u>Acknowledgment.</u> As could clearly be seen through the prelimi-
nary activities, responsive listeners are essential for a successful interaction. Even if they have nothing to add to the
point, listeners must acknowledge verbally what the speaker has
said in order to show that they have understood and that they
are interested and ready to initiate repair if needed. The
following activity is an excellent warmup at the beginning of
class. The teacher announces a real or invented "news" item and
elicits reactions from the group in the form of partial repetitions or surprise markers (see no. 18).

Example: Wißt ihr was? Heute morgen auf dem Weg zur Schule
habe ich einen $50 Schein gefunden!--Was? $50? Heute
morgen? Tatsächlich?

Vous savez quoi? Ce matin en venant à l'école j'ai
trouvé un billet de $50 dans la rue!--Quoi? $50? Ce
matin? Ce n'est pas vrai!

(Do you know what? This morning on the way to school I
found a $50 bill!--What? This morning? $50? No kidding!)

Or each student comes to class with a news item and announces it
to the class or to a neighbor, who in turn expresses surprise
and interest.

51

Variation: Students work in pairs. Student A tells B about the latest film he or she saw, or about the essay he or she wrote for that day. Student B has to encourage the speaker with cues listed under nos. 17 or 18. It is interesting to observe how a little verbal encouragement and sympathy on the part of the listener can really make a difference for the speaker and create a climate of friendship and care in the classroom.

Giving in/Terminating an argument. Students often run out of things to say but don't know how to terminate the conversation, so they either repeat themselves or just stop talking. The following exercise practices concluding an argument. Work in pairs. Student A makes up a request to which Student B replies without much enthusiasm, using "hesitation openers" (no. 1.4). Student A then adds an offer that is too good to refuse, so B changes his or her mind by using one of the "giving in" cues (no. 19.3).

Example: A: Kannst du mir helfen, mein Zimmer sauber zu machen?
           B: Na ja, weißt du, ich habe nicht so viel Zeit.
           A: Ich gebe dir 5 Dollar die Stunde.
           B: Also gut.

           A: Tu peux m'aider à ranger ma chambre?
           B: Ben, c'est-à-dire, tu sais, je n'ai pas vraiment le
              temps.
           A: Je te donnerai 5 dollars de l'heure.
           B: Bon, si tu veux, d'accord.

   (A: Can you help me clean up my room? B: Well, you know, I
   don't have that much time. A: I'll give you $5 an hour.
   B: O.K., then.)

The same strategy can be used to terminate the visit of the insistent salesperson in the counter-argument (p. 49) game or to end any of the persuasion games (see below).

Fighting back. If teachers misinterpret what students have said, the students generally think they were wrong and that their teachers know better. In natural conversation, students must learn how to protest to fellow students who have misrepresented something they have said. Hence the following exercise: the teacher acts as if he or she was hard of hearing and consistently repeats what the students say, including mistakes and misunderstandings. The students have to fight back immediately and correct the teacher with one of the cues listed under no. 22.

Buying Time

This is a major skill, which should be mastered for all conversations, when speakers take the floor with hesitation, when

52

they need a few seconds to formulate and organize their thoughts
without losing the floor, when they repeat someone else's statement, or when they have no definite opinion about a matter. The
interview game puts all these hesitation markers into play (see
nos. 1.4, 10.1-10.4). An interview board consisting of two or
three students should make a list of difficult interview questions for a job that they define. All other students are applicants for the job and are interviewed one after the other.
Applicants are understandably nervous and must punctuate their
answers with such cues as na ja, ja also, tja; wie soll ich
sagen, sag'n wir mal; irgendwie; im Grunde, eigentlich/ bon...
ben, vous savez, c'est-à-dire; comment dire; disons, si vous
voulez; au fond, en fait, enfin (well, you know, of course; you
know what I mean; actually, practically, basically).

Examples of questions:

Warum wollen Sie Ihre jetzige Stelle verlassen?/ Pourquoi
voulez-vous quitter l'emploi que vous avez actuellement?
(Why do you want to leave your present job?)

Warum wollen Sie diese Arbeit haben?/ Pourquoi vous
intéressez-vous à ce poste? (Why do you want this job?)

Wie stellen Sie sich Ihr Leben in zehn Jahren vor?/ Quels
sont vos projets d'avenir? (How do you picture your life
ten years from now?)

This activity may be combined with an exercise in paraphrasing
(see Appendix 1).

Mitigation

Many linguistic markers that serve to buy time are also used
as mitigators. By moderating a statement, speakers make themselves less vulnerable to counter-arguments. Students must be
able to (1) reformulate a strong statement with such cues as das
heißt, beziehungsweise, ich meine/ ou plutôt, ou si vous voulez,
disons (that is, let us say, or rather, I mean); (2) mitigate an
adjective or a verb with phrases like gewißermaßen, in gewißem
Sinne/ en quelque sorte, pour ainsi dire (so to speak, more or
less, practically); (3) show honesty by prefacing their remarks
with es kommt darauf an, tja das ist eben die Frage/ ça dépend,
ben tout dépend de (it depends; well, that's the question).
Here are a few extreme statements that one sometimes makes for
lack of better words. Extricate yourself, using the cue in
parentheses (taken from 6.5, 10.3, 21.1, and 21.2) to add a mitigating statement.

1. Ich brauche kein Wörterbuch (das heißt)/ Je ne me sers
   jamais d'un dictionnaire (c'est-à-dire) (I never use a dic-
   tionary--that is)

2. Ich rauche nie (beziehungsweise)/ Je ne fume jamais (ou disons) (I never smoke, or let us say)

3. Frauen sind schlechte Autofahrer (beziehungsweise es kommt darauf an:)/ Les femmes conduisent mal (enfin, ça dépend:) (Women are bad drivers, or rather it depends:)

4. Ärzte bekommen nicht genug bezahlt (ich meine)/ Les medecins ne sont pas assez payés (ou si vous voulez) (Doctors are not paid enough, I mean)

Debates and Discussions

The following are games and argumentative activities that put into play all the conversational skills practiced above. They can be classified into two major groups, using the logician's distinction between debate and discussion. According to Perelman (1970), a debate is a search for victory between one of two opposite viewpoints through the use of skills of persuasion. Its main strategies are those of demonstration based on evidence that is gathered and presented. By contrast, a discussion is a search for the truth or the best solution to a problem through the use of skills of conviction. Its main strategies are those of argumentation based on a sincere interest in the other speaker's opinion and a desire to attain a compromise by making a choice between possible solutions. The following activities are listed in increasing degree of interaction and cooperation.

Games of Persuasion

Color clash. Players work in pairs, each partner choosing his or her favorite color. Within a time limit of several minutes, players must try to persuade their opposite that their own color is far better. Any arguments or means of persuasion can be used. Davison and Gordon (1978)[3] note that "this game sounds straightforward, but many groups find that as they try to persuade the other person, they become more convinced of the validity of their own color; then more complex arguments are generated." It is often the case that students start repeating previous arguments if they run out of new ones. To ensure progression and victory, one may add the rule that the first partner to repeat an argument in the same form as before loses the game.

Hard sell. Students draw their "dream car" on a piece of paper. They are then told that the president of their college or school has decided to buy a car for each member of the faculty but has not yet decided on the model. The class divides into "presidents" and "salespeople." Each salesperson has to persuade each president to select his or her model. They then reverse roles. The presidents drive a hard bargain, and the salespeople use all their discursive skills to "manage" the sale.

<u>Gentle persuasion</u>. In pairs, students role-play the following
situations:

1. Herr Meier/M. Durand and his wife arrive at the theater
    before the curtain goes up. They find two other persons
    sitting in their seats. They try to persuade them that
    these seats are theirs and that they have to go elsewhere.
    They meet with great resistance, and both parties have to
    find a solution to this awkward situation.

2. Herr Schulze/M. Dupont has put a marriage ad in the news-
    paper. He has received many answers. He has agreed to meet
    one of the respondents in a restaurant. She tries to per-
    suade him that she is just the woman he needs. He lets him-
    self be persuaded or not. Time limit: five minutes.

<u>More persuasion</u>. In pairs, students are given three or four
minutes to role-play the following:

1. Persuade your parents to turn the TV to a program you
    want to watch.

2. Persuade your brother to lend you something.

3. Persuade your father to increase your pocket money.

4. Persuade your grandmother who lives with you to go away
    for the weekend with your parents so that you can have a
    party.

5. Persuade the bus conductor to let you travel home for
    free.

(The persuasion is met in each case with some resistance.)

<u>Group persuasion</u>. One student ("Mary") is told she has to stay
home tonight. Under no circumstances is she to allow herself to
be persuaded to leave the house. It is up to her to decide on
her reason for wanting to be alone and not go out. The other
students are all related to her in some way (business colleague,
dentist, neighbor, daughter, father, mother, mother-in-law,
etc.), and time is given for them to decide who they are and to
think of a valid reason and method for getting her out of the
house. They succeed as soon as Mary cannot offer any new reason
for staying in the house.

Debates

<u>Pro and con</u>. This first series of debates trains students to
relate their point to what another speaker has just said. Students work in triads. Each triad consists of two participants

and one referee. The participants agree to discuss a topic of mutual interest and to defend opposite viewpoints:

1. Zensuren: gut oder schlecht?/ les notes: bon ou mauvais système? (grades: good or bad?)

2. Frauencolleges oder gemischte Colleges?/ collèges de femmes ou collèges mixtes? (women's colleges or co-ed?)

3. Studentenheime: getrennt oder gemischt?/ maisons d'étudiants: séparées ou mixtes? (dorms: separate or co-ed?)

4. Ladendiebstahl: zulässig oder unzulässig?/ les vols dans les supermarchés: excusables ou non? (shoplifting: acceptable or not?)

5. Zoos und Zirkusse: pro und contra/ les zoos et les cirques: pour et contre (zoos and circuses: for and against)

6. Die Mode: Vor- und Nachteile/ la mode: avantages et inconvénients (fashion: advantages and disadvantages)

7. Die Todesstrafe: notwendig oder nicht?/ la peine capitale: nécessaire ou non? (capital punishment: necessary or not?)

8. Drogen zur Erhöhung der Intelligenz: für und wider/ les drogues pour hausser le niveau de l'intelligence: pour ou contre? (drugs to increase intelligence: for or against?)

Individual participants start the conversation and attempt to convince the listener of their position. Once they are finished, the second participant attempts to summarize or wind up the first participant's statements. The accuracy of the summary is judged both by the referee and the other participant. If the summary is satisfactory, the second participant then offers his or her views persuasively on the subject. The first participant must then summarize the statements to the satisfaction of the two other students. All three students should have a chance in turn to be both a participant and a referee.

Personal viewpoints. A whole-group activity. Each student is given an index card containing one opinion opener and one responder. These discursive devices give each student—even the more silent ones—easier access to the conversational "pool." The students must use their markers to take the floor and preface their statement within the time limit set by the teacher for

56

the debate. According to the level of proficiency of the class, these markers can be short or long, and each card can contain one, two, or three of them. For the next debate, students switch cards. The markers may be either read or memorized. Suggested topics:

1. Soll das Mädchen bezahlen, wenn sie mit einem Jungen ausgeht?/ Qui doit payer quand un jeune homme sort avec une jeune fille? (Who should pay for the date, the boy or the girl?)

2. Sollten Zensuren abgeschafft werden?/ Devrait-on éliminer les notes à l'école? (Should grades be eliminated?)

3. Ist die Euthanasie gerechtfertigt?/ L'euthanasie est-elle justifiable? (Is euthanasia justified?)

4. Sollten ausländische Studenten arbeiten dürfen, während sie in Amerika studieren, um ihr Studium zu finanzieren?/ Les étudiants étrangers en Amérique devraient-ils avoir le droit de travailler pour financer leurs études? (Should foreign students in the U.S. be allowed to work to finance their studies?)

5. Was ist das ideale Heiratsalter?/ Quel est l'âge idéal pour se marier? (What is the ideal marrying age?)

6. Sollte Sexualkunde in der Schule unterrichtet werden?/ Devrait-il y avoir des cours d'éducation sexuelle dans les écoles secondaires? (Should sex education be given in secondary schools?)

7. Sollten Eheverträge nur für fünf Jahre abgeschlossen werden?/ Devrait-il y avoir des contrats de mariage pour cinq ans seulement? (Should marriage contracts be given only for five years?)

Shock slogans. In groups of two or with the whole class, the following shock statements can be argued and extreme viewpoints ventilated. Students generally enjoy arguing the most extreme positions and "winning" purely on their rhetoric. They prepare their arguments and the necessary vocabulary in advance.

1. Lehrer haben zu viele Ferien./ Les professeurs ont trop de vacances. (Teachers have too much vacation.)

2. Die Schule bereitet einen gar nicht auf das Leben vor./ L'école ne vous prépare pas à la vie. (School does not prepare you for life.)

3. Die medizinische Betreuung sollte in den USA kostenlos sein./ Les soins médicaux devraient être gratuits aux USA. (Medical care in the U.S. should be free.)

4. Das Leben fängt mit 40 an./ La vie commence à 40 ans. (Life begins at 40.)

5. Gewalttätigkeit im Fernsehen ist etwas Schönes./ La violence à la télé est une bonne chose. (Violence on TV is a good thing.)

Discussions

Unlike debates, discussions aim at a group solution of a given problem or difficult situation, and agreement on a course of action. The skills needed here are more argumentative than demonstrative, and practice is provided for interaction in task-oriented situations.

Decision making. You are going to Germany/France for a year. Since you are afraid that your luggage might get lost, you want to put into a handbag 15 items you will absolutely need there. In groups of three, students have 15 minutes to make up their list and rank the items in order of importance. The lists can then be compared and justified.

You are spending your vacation in Germany/France with a friend. All hotels in town and the youth hostel are full. Decide with your friend where and how you are going to spend the night (four minutes).

Individual claims. Students return to their partners an object they borrowed and that they are returning in less than perfect condition. The borrowers have two minutes to decide on an object and invent an excuse. They then have to apologize and give explanations; the owners have to offer a way in which the situation can be repaired, and both owners and borrowers have to come to an agreement.

Family circle. Students write on a piece of paper some trouble that they were actually or fictitiously involved in at school, at home, with the neighbors, or with friends. Papers are then redistributed at random among the group. In "family" groups of three, the students then have to discuss these problems and agree on a course of action.

Collective bargaining. Students get together to set up a list of grievances, e.g., to improve study conditions at their school, schedules, food, etc. They are to bring their grievances to a panel of three students: the grievance committee. They decide which group is going to present which particular grievance. They set up a list of suggestions and alternatives to be discussed. Both parties then bargain for a common decision. Examples:

1. Schlechtes Essen in der Mensa/ la mauvaise qualité de la nourriture à la cantine (bad food in the cafeteria)

2. Eine Autobahn wird neben der Schule gebaut./ On est en train de construire une autoroute près de l'école. (A highway is being built near the school.)

3. Der Deutschkurs entspricht nicht den Erwartungen./ Le cours de français ne répond pas aux besoins des étudiants. (The German/French class does not meet the expectations of the students.)

The same game can be played with two parties involved and an arbiter or referee.

Example:

Eine neue Diskothek hat gerade auf Ihrer Straße aufgemacht. Zusammen mit ein paar Nachbarn gehen Sie zum Bürgermeister, um sich zu beklagen. Der Inhaber der Diskothek ist auch dabei. Beide Parteien verteidigen ihren Standpunkt. Ihre Klagen sind unter anderem: zuviel Lärm bis 4 Uhr morgens; zuviel Radau auf der Straße; Verpestung der Luft durch die Motorräder; mögliche Gewalttätigkeiten durch betrunkene Jugendliche usw. Der Inhaber der Diskothek verteidigt seine Interessen und die Interessen der Jugendlichen. Sie kommen eventuell zu folgendem Kompromiss: bessere Isolierung des Lokals; strikt eingehaltene Öffnungszeiten; Motorräder auf der Straße verboten; polizeiliche Überwachung der Straße; Probezeit: 1 Monat.

On vient d'ouvrir une nouvelle discothèque dans votre rue. Vous vous joignez à un groupe de vos voisins pour aller porter plainte à la mairie. Le propriétaire de la discothèque s'y trouve aussi. Les deux partis défendent leur point de vue devant le maire. Le propriétaire de la discothèque défend ses intérêts et ceux des jeunes. Vos griefs sont, entre autres: bruit assourdissant de la musique jusqu'à 4h du matin; trop de bruit dans la rue; pollution de l'air par les motos; attitude agressive des jeunes; scènes d'ivresse et de violence. Le maire arbitre la confrontation. On pourra arriver aux solutions de compromis suivantes: meilleure isolation acoustique du local; respect des horaires de fermeture; fermeture de la rue aux motocyclettes; présence d'un agent de police dans la rue; mise à l'épreuve d'un mois.

(A new discotheque has opened on your street. Together with a few neighbors you go to the mayor and complain. The owner of the discotheque is there. Both parties defend their position. The owner defends his interests and the interests of the young people. Some of your complaints might be: too much noise until 4 a.m.; too much rowdiness on the street; air pollution from the exhaust of the motorcycles; possibility of violence by drunk teenagers, etc. You might reach the following compromise: improved acoustic insulation of the building; strict enforcement of opening and closing hours; prohibition of motorcycles on that street; police patrol on the street; probation time: 1 month.)

Other possible conflict situations:

1. Ein Kinderspielplatz wird gebaut./ construction d'un parc de jeux pour enfants (building a new playground)

2. Parkuhren werden auf Ihrer Straße aufgestellt./ installation de parc-mètres dans votre rue (installation of parking meters on your street)

3. Ein Supermarkt wird in Ihrer Nachbarschaft gebaut./ construction d'un supermarché dans votre quartier (building a supermarket in your neighborhood)

4. Ein Miethaus wird abgerissen, um ein neues Studentenheim zu bauen./ démolition d'un immeuble pour construire une maison d'étudiants (tearing down an apartment building to build a new student dorm)

*   *   *

The discursive approach to the teaching of language suggested in this paper actualizes recent thought in sociolinguistics, discourse analysis, and foreign language pedagogy. Although the emphasis here has been placed on the interactive oral skills, it is clear that many of the strategies presented have their counterparts in written language. Students can be taught in the same manner to organize written discourse and to understand the interaction between writer and reader.

In the classroom, students are traditionally taught how to listen and how to speak, not how to interact. The study of the rules of natural interaction and of the construction of discourse can be extremely fruitful for effective foreign language teaching. Much work still needs to be done, however, in this direction. We need a topology of discourse operations or discourse grammar. We need comparative studies of the cultural elements of discourse. Moreover, we need a new role for foreign language teachers. They must be ready to teach the students precisely those strategies that account for much of their own "fluency" in the classroom. The exercises suggested in this study must be viewed as part of training in autonomous learning. If not, they will be tedious and meaningless "gambits." The primary role of teachers should become that of managers of discourse rather than managers of knowledge, and they should teach their students how to manage their own learning by "talking like the teacher."

Hesitating and Expanding

Step 1: Observation (German)

The following is an authentic conversation between two German
natives. Listen carefully to the way A and B "manage" the conversation. A is an interviewer, B a young apprentice. Note B's
hesitation strategies. Underline all the statements made by A
which are <u>not</u> direct questions. Note their function. Observe
how B builds on A's paraphrases and restatements.

B: Ich arbeite in der Metallindustrie.

A: Ja. Warum haben Sie gerade diesen Beruf
    gewählt? Also Metallindustrie?

(hesitation B: Das war eigentlich irgendwie auch mal mit
fillers)   (pause) mein Traumberuf war: ich wollte gerne
                    arbeiten und zwar nicht gerade geistig sondern
                    mehr körperlich.

(making   A: Ja. Also kann man sagen, daß Sie ihn selbst
inferences)   gewählt haben diesen Beruf.

              B: Ich habe diesen Beruf selbst gewählt.

              A: Ja. Und was macht zum Beispiel Ihr Vater?
                  Und ist Ihre Mutter auch berufstätig?

              B: Nein. Meine Mutter ist nicht berufstätig,
                  aber mein Vater ist Vermessungsingenieur im
                  öffentlichen Dienst.

(request   A: Ja. Können Sie das vielleicht etwas näher
for clari-   erklären was das ist ein Vermessungsingenieur?
fication)

              B: Ein Vermessungsingenieur das ist (pause) im
                  öffentlichen Dienst, das wär (pause) bei der
                  Bundeswehr (pause) er vermißt sozusagen die
                  Landkarten, die ja auch später hergestellt
                  werden.

              A: Ja, ja. Leben Sie noch bei Ihren Eltern?

              B: Ja, ich lebe noch bei meinen Eltern (pause)
                  aber (pause)

(guessing, A: Es gefällt Ihnen nicht mehr so recht.
completing)
              B: Es gefällt mir nicht, weil (pause) ich dement-

62

sprechend (pause) noch mehr Aufgaben zu Hause
zu erledigen habe.

(suggesting   A: Ja müssen Sie da helfen (pause) oder (pause)
interpreta-
tion)
                 B: Helfen weniger, aber es fallen so Arbeiten an,
                     wie Reparaturen, die so im Haushalt vorkommen.

(making   A: Hm, hm. Und Sie würden also vielleicht lieber
inferences)   allein wohnen und unabhängig sein?

                 B: Allein wohnen schon, aber ganz unabhängig
                     (pause) das, glaub' ich, ist in meinem Alter
                     noch zu früh.

(suggesting   A: Ja. Und vielleicht ist Ihr Einkommen auch
causes)   nicht so hoch. Wieviel verdient so ein Lehr-
                     ling?

                 B: Also....[5]

Step 2: Analysis

Hesitation Strategies	Expansion Strategies
Ja also	Contextual guessing and completion of sentences
Also	
	Making inferences
Sozusagen	
	Offering interpretation
Eigentlich	
	Suggesting causes
Irgendwie	
	Requesting clarification

Step 3: Practice

Switching modes. The question/answer/question/answer pattern of
discourse might be appropriate for an inquiry in court or a
grammar drill, but it is highly unnatural for a conversational
interaction. Role-play a conversation between a reporter and a
famous person of your choice. As a reporter, you want to learn
as much as you can about the person in order to write a good
article, but you want to win the trust of the interviewee by
asking as few direct questions as possible. See how long you
can go with expansion strategies before you ask your next question. As an interviewee, you will need hesitation markers to
give yourself time to think.

Step 1: Observation (French)

The following is an authentic conversation between two French natives. Listen carefully to the way J and B "manage" the conversation. J is an interviewer, B a young hairdresser. Double slashes indicate longer pauses; dots are used wherever the original text has been shortened for demonstration purposes. Note B's hesitation strategies. Underline all the statements made by J which are <u>not</u> direct questions. Note their function. Observe how B builds on J's paraphrases and restatements.

J: Et quelle sorte de client préférez-vous?

B: Écoutez, le, la clientèle que je préfère, en fait, c'est la clientèle, euh, disons, euh, assez aisée (J: Oui) notamment

(suggesting causes)

J: Parce que, parce que cette clientèle donne des pourboires plus généreux?

(hesitations)

B: Peut-être, peut-être, hein? Elle est plus généreuse que la clientèle de bureau c'est sûr, de par leur situation. Et en plus on a des, si vous voulez, des discussions qui sont quand même beaucoup plus // (on se reçoit mutuellement chez soi) // qu'avec la cliente de bureau, bon, elle est beaucoup plus son travail, que celle qui ne travaille pas, en fait. Et on a moins l'occasion de se recevoir. Moi, avec mes clientes qui ne travaillent pas, on se reçoit très souvent. Disons qu'elles me reçoivent très souvent chez elles (J: Oui) ne serait-ce que pour les coiffer à domicile....

(making inferences)

J: Oui, donc.

B: Alors on aura plus de contact.

(restatement, summing up)

J: Pour vous la coiffure ce n'est pas seulement, euh, rendre, euh, changer l'apparence de vos, de vos clientes, faire une oeuvre de, esthétique, mais c'est aussi

B: Un contact.

(completion of sentences)

J: Un contact humain.

B: C'est aussi un contact humain.

(paraphrase offering interpretation)

J: Et les, les, les rapports que vous pouvez établir entre vous et vos clients.

Oui, absolument, absolument. C'est ce qui
est d'ailleurs très intéressant.

(four   J: Mais tout de même est-ce que vous avez jamais
paraphrases   eu une situation désagréable, c'est-à-dire
for greater   que quelqu'un qui vraiment une cliente qui
specificity)   vraiment était désagréable, qui, qui vous a
causé un problème, qui vraiment où vous étiez
mal à l'aise, vous étiez gênée?

B: Ben, j'ai des clientes capricieuses, euh, qui
aiment bien qu'on s'occupe d'elles et qui
n'aiment pas attendre, euh, quand elles ont
// moi j'ai eu des clientes par exemple qui
viennent toutes les semaines au salon se
coiffer.[6]

Step 2: Analysis

Hesitation Strategies	Expansion Strategies

En fait

Disons

...hein?

Si vous voulez

Bon

Ben

Euh

Expansion Strategies content:

Contextual guessing and completion
of sentences

Making inferences

Equivalent paraphrases to offer
interpretation

Suggesting causes

Paraphrases summing up previous
statement

Series of paraphrases for greater
specificity

Step 3: Practice

(See Step 3 under German.)

Some Conversational Management Strategies Used by
French and German Native Speakers*

    The following strategies of spoken language have their counterparts in those used by American speakers of English to manage conversations. The English markers are equivalents, not translations, of the French and the German.

    Although many conversational strategies are common to all three languages and cultures, some strategies are used more in one and less in the other. For example, it seems that French speakers check the attention and the understanding of their listener much more often than Germans or Americans do. In addition, they have a predilection for the dramatic effects achieved by the repetition of the first or last elements of a sentence. By contrast, it seems that German speakers favor a more "epic" kind of delivery. Their speech shows a much higher incidence of prefacing and priming strategies and a higher rate of syntactic articulation. Americans seem to have in comparison a rather "dynamic" style of delivery that does without many of the linguistic markers used by the French and the Germans. A cross-cultural comparison of discourse patterns would go beyond the scope of this study, but undoubtedly this is a field that needs to be explored.

    The equivalent markers thus given for each category can only be approximations, pending a more in-depth cultural study of the discursive features of each language. The degree of formality or informality of each marker is indicated as follows:

                neutral: o
                informal: -
                formal: +

Examples from the spoken language are given whenever usage is complex.

---

*This list of "gambits" is far from being exhaustive, but it offers the non-native teacher a useful starting point. Slashes indicate alternative gambits or elements of gambits, parentheses offer possible additions. The position of the predicates in the statements that would follow the German gambits is (1) at the end of the dependent clause if introduced by daß, (2) in second position (as in a main clause) if introduced by a colon. Elsewhere syntactic usage is indicated or made clear through examples. For the French markers, whenever the subjunctive is required after the gambit, this is indicated in parentheses. Otherwise the verb is in the indicative.

Taking the Floor (Turn Taking)

1. Attention Getting

1.1 Polite interrupting

-    Moment.
o   Entschuldigung:
o   Also ich muß sagen:
o   Ich hätte mal eine Frage:
+   Darf ich einen Moment unterbrechen:

-    Une minute.
o   Pardon./ Je m'excuse.
o   J'aimerais dire une chose:
o   J'aimerais savoir:
+   Si vous permettez:

(Wait a minute; Excuse me; I'd like to say something; I'd
like to ask something; I have a question; May I say something?)

1.2 Impatient interrupting

-    Moment mal!
-    Also pass mal auf:
-    (Jetzt) Schau mal:/ Hör mal:/ Sag mal:/ Also:
o   Einen Moment!
+   Ich darf doch jetzt einen Moment unterbrechen:

-    Attends!
-    Ah mais attention!/ Ah mais pardon!/ Mais enfin:
-    Non mais écoute:/ Regarde:/ Attends:/ Tiens:
o   Alors là:
+   Tu permets:

(Hold it! Just a minute! Well now listen; Look; Hey!
Excuse me for interrupting.)

1.3 Interrupting to add a point

-    Da möchte ich sagen:
o   Also ich würde sagen/meinen:
o   Also da kann ich nur sagen:
o   Jetzt muß ich aber etwas sagen:
+   Darf ich dazu etwas sagen:

-    Il y a en plus le fait que
-    Tout ce que je sais c'est que
o   J'aimerais aussi dire une chose/ajouter une chose, c'est
que

67

o   Il faut aussi dire une chose, c'est que
+   Je voudrais signaler à ce propos que

(I'd like to add/say here that; I'd like to make a point; I might add here; All I can say is; Now I have to say that)

1.4 Hesitation openers (also for buying time and mitigation)

-    Tja
-    Hör' mal:
-    Na ja
o   Ja/nun also:
o   Ja weißt du:
o   Was soll ich sagen/ wie soll ich sagen:

-    Bon ben
-    Ben tu sais/tu vois
-    Ben, comment dire
o   Eh bien, c'est-à-dire que
o   Si tu veux
o   En fait

(Well; Well you see/you know; Well now of course; Look/listen; What can I say? How shall I put it?)

2. Opinion Opening

2.1 Simple opinion

o   (Also) Ich finde/meine/muß sagen:
o   Ich meine (einfach):
o   Ich bin der Meinung:
o   Meiner Meinung nach/ meiner Ansicht nach, (+ verb)
o   An deiner Stelle würde ich
+   Für meine Begriffe
+   ...meines Erachtens
+   ...nach meiner Auffassung/ nach meinem Dafürhalten

o   (Moi) Je trouve/je pense/je crois/j'estime que
o   Je suis d'avis que
o   Il me semble que
o   A mon avis/ à mon sens
o   Mon idée c'est que
o   Si j'étais toi, je
+   D'après moi/ selon moi
+   Pour ma part, je pense que

([Well] I think/feel/believe/have to say that; It seems to me; In my opinion/my view; My understanding is; As I see it/ understand it; If I were you; To my mind)

2.2 Well-grounded opinion

- o   Es ist doch klar, daß
- o   Selbstverständlich finde ich, daß
- o   Es liegt doch auf der Hand, daß
- o   Ich kann nur eins sagen:
- +   Ich bin durchaus der Meinung, daß

- o   Il est clair/évident que
- o   Il va de soi que
- o   Franchement, je trouve que
- o   Ce que je veux dire, c'est que
- +   Mon opinion/mon point de vue, c'est que

(It is clear/obvious that; Clearly/obviously; I honestly feel that; What I want to say is that; It is my opinion that)

2.3 Firm conviction (emphatic)

- o   Ich bin (fest) davon überzeugt, daß
- o   Es ist von vornherein klar, daß
- o   Da kann ich nur folgendes sagen:
- +   Ich bin der festen Überzeugung, daß
- +   Ich stehe auf dem Standpunkt, daß
- +   Ich vertrete den Standpunkt/die Auffassung, daß

- o   Je suis fermement/absolument persuadé/convaincu/sûr/ certain que
- o   Il est absolument certain que
- o   Il est indéniable que
- o   Il n'y a pas de doute/il n'y a aucun doute que
- o   Ca ne fait pas de doute que
- o   Tout ce que je peux dire, c'est que

(I can only say one thing; I am absolutely/firmly convinced/ positive that; My position on the matter is; My views on the subject are; I strongly believe that; It is clear from the start that)

2.4 Personal stand

- −   Also von mir aus, (+ verb)
- o   Also ich kann nur sagen:
- o   Also für mich persönlich (+ verb)
- +   Ich persönlich bin der Meinung:
- +   Wenn du mich nach meiner persönlichen Meinung fragst:

- −   En ce qui me concerne:
- −   Alors moi là je dis:

o   Si tu veux mon avis
o   Moi personnellement je trouve/je pense que

(I personally believe/feel that; As far as I'm concerned;
If you want my personal opinion; In my personal opinion)

3. Framing and Focusing

3.1 Simple

o   Die Hauptsache ist:
o   Ich gehe (erst mal) davon aus: (+ direct question)
o   Die (eigentliche) Frage ist (nämlich) die:
o   Die Frage ist, daß
o   Wir wollen einfach fragen: (+ direct question)
+   Das ist ein wichtiger Punkt:
+   Etwas (vor allem), was betont werden muß:
+   Wir müssen zuerst mal feststellen:

o   (Pour moi) L'essentiel c'est que (+ subjunctive)
o   La chose la plus importante c'est
o   Ce qui est important, c'est de savoir
o   Il faut bien se demander
o   Le problème c'est que/ c'est justement là la question
o   Il faudrait d'abord savoir si
+   Ca c'est un point très important
+   Il faut bien souligner que

([For me] the most important thing is; That is an important
point; The real question/problem is; This is the whole
point/problem/question; It is (primarily) a question of; My
first question is:; That's a good question/point; That's
precisely the point.)

3.2 Emphatic

o   Es geht (im Grunde) doch nur um eins:/um die Frage:
o   Im Grunde kommt es (nur) darauf an
o   Man muß sich darüber klar sein, daß
o   Es geht doch (hauptsächlich/im wesentlichen/vor allem/
    vor allen Dingen) darum, daß
+   Es läuft alles auf die Frage hin:
+   Hier liegt für mich der entscheidende Punkt:
+   Das scheint mir ein ganz wichtiger Punkt zu sein:

o   (Au fond) il s'agit/ c'est (avant tout/surtout/princi-
    palement/essentiellement) une question de
o   (En fait/au fond) C'est là le point le plus important:
o   Il y a une chose de certaine c'est que
o   Il y a une chose qui me semble extrêmement importante:

70

(It is basically/essentially/mainly/primarily a question of;
In fact, the only important point is; The crux of the matter
is; It all boils down to the problem of; This brings up the
problem of; That is an extremely important point.)

4. Redirecting the Topic

4.1 Side track

- Außerdem
- Übrigens
o Im übrigen

- D'ailleurs
- A propos

(By the way)

4.2 Association

- A propos X
o Wenn wir schon von X reden:

- A propos de X/ parlant de X
- Pour en revenir à X
o A ce sujet

(That reminds me; Speaking of X)

4.3 Introducing entirely new aspect

- Und wie ist es mit X?

- Une question: (+ direct question)

(And what about X? How about X?)

Keeping the Floor (Internal Organization
of the Turn-at-Talk)

5. Self-Paraphrasing

5.1 With repetition of first element

Es ist nicht sicher, daß ich heirate, es ist nicht sicher,
daß ich mich nicht scheiden lasse, es ist nicht sicher, daß
meine Ehe gut geht, deswegen ist es auf jeden Fall wichtig,
daß ich einen Beruf habe. (It's not certain that I will
marry, it's not certain that I won't get divorced, it's not

certain that my marriage will work out, so in any case it is
important that I have a job.)

C'est très important de savoir ce que l'on désire voir dans
un pays, ce que l'on désire apprendre. Chacun peut venir
discuter des problèmes qu'il a, des problèmes qu'il rencontre. (It is very important to know what you want to see
in a country, what you want to learn. Everyone can come and
discuss the problems he has, the problems he encounters.)

5.2 With repetition of last element

Ich wollte mich selbständig machen, ich habe mich
selbständig gemacht. (I wanted to become independent, I
became independent.)

Je veux m'installer. Je cherche à m'installer. Je cherche
un local commercial pour m'installer. (I want to settle
down. I am looking into settling down. I am looking for a
place to settle down.)

5.3 With increasing specificity

Man muß seinen Sohn darüber aufklären, wie er sich in der
Gesellschaft, mit seinen Eltern, mit seinen Freunden, auch
wie er sich gegenüber dem anderen Geschlecht verhalten soll.
(You have to teach your son how to behave in society, how to
behave with his parents, his friends, and how to behave with
girls.)

Il y a eu très peu de scandales dans la coiffure, très peu
de gens qui protestent, qui font appel au syndicat ou qui se
mettent en grève. (There have been very few scandals in the
hairdressing business; very few people have protested,
involved the trade union, or gone on strike.)

5.4 With increasing generality

Die Kinder können spielen, die können sich entfalten, die
können alles machen, die haben kaum Einschränkungen. (The
children can play, they can develop freely, they can do
everything--they have hardly any restrictions.)

Pour bien connaître les Français, il faut savoir comment ils
mangent, comment ils parlent, il faut connaître leurs habi-
tudes, leur style de vie, tout leur héritage culturel et
social. (To know the French, you have to know how they eat,
how they speak; you have to know their habits, their life-
style, their whole cultural and social background.)

5.5 Synonymies for greater clarification or emphasis

Haben Sie ein Vorbild, ein Leitbild, ein Traumbild, gibt es
einen Menschen in Ihrem Bekanntenkreis, dessen Leben Sie
nachvollziehen möchten? (Do you have a model, someone you
admire, someone you dream of being like, is there someone
you know whose life you would like to imitate?)

Tu sais déjà ce que tu veux devenir plus tard, tu as une
idée du genre de travail que tu aimerais faire? (Do you
know what you want to become later in life, do you have any
idea of the kind of work you would like to do?)

5.6 Repetition of own or of other's statement

A: Sie haben ihn selbst gewählt, diesen Beruf?
B: Ich habe diesen Beruf selbst gewählt.
(A: So you chose that profession yourself? B: I chose this
profession myself.)

A: La télé, c'est tout pour nous.
B: Ah bon.
A: Ah oui, la télé, c'est tout pour nous.
(A: TV is everything for us. B: Ah ha. A: Yes, TV is
everything for us.)

6. Expanding a Point

6.1 Explanation/clarification

Also/ das heißt/ ich meine
A savoir/ c'est-à-dire/ je veux dire
(That is; i.e.; I mean; namely)

Es dauert sehr lange, also praktisch zwei Stunden. (It
takes a long time, i.e., roughly two hours.)

Heiraten muß man aus Liebe, also zu dem Mann nicht zum
Geschlechtsverkehr. (One should marry for love--love for
the man, that is, not for sex.)

Des conseils techniques, c'est-à-dire des conseils cinémato-
graphiques ou photographiques, des conseils pratiques.
(Technical advice, I mean, advice concerning films and
cameras, practical advice.)

6.2 Specification

Und zwar/nämlich/in dem Sinne daß
(Namely; and indeed; in the sense that)

Ich war als Hilfspfleger tätig, <u>und</u> <u>zwar</u> vor allen Dingen aus dem Grunde (I was working as an assistant nurse [namely] mainly because)

Das finde ich sehr interessant, <u>und</u> <u>zwar</u> (I find this very interesting, namely)

Wir sind hier bei einem schwierigen Problem, <u>nämlich</u> wir diskutieren über eine Frage, die noch gar nicht entscheidbar ist. (We are faced here with a difficult problem, namely, one for which there is as yet no solution.)

6.3 Amplification

Nicht nur <u>X</u>, sondern auch <u>Y</u>/ sowohl <u>X</u>...als auch <u>Y</u>/ einerseits...andererseits

D'abord <u>X</u>...et puis <u>Y</u>/ d'abord <u>X</u>...ensuite <u>Y</u>/ d'un côté... d'un autre côté

(Both <u>X</u> and <u>Y</u>; Not only <u>X</u>, but also <u>Y</u>; <u>X</u> as well as <u>Y</u>; On the one hand...on the other hand)

Und das <u>nicht</u> <u>nur</u> im Rheinland <u>sondern</u> <u>auch</u> in Westfalen und anderen Gebieten. (And this applies both to the Rhineland and to Westfalia and other areas.)

Große Chancen haben sich heute eröffnet in der Behandlung <u>einerseits</u> durch die Heilkrampfbehandlung, <u>andererseits</u> aber vor allem durch die Psychopharmaka. (Great possibilities have become available nowadays for the treatment of [mental disorders], on the one hand through electroshock therapy, and on the other hand especially through the use of drugs.)

Un milieu bourgeois c'est un milieu <u>d'abord</u> dans lequel il y a des traditions...<u>et</u> <u>puis</u> surtout où il y a relativement de l'argent. (A bourgeois milieu is a milieu with traditions, and of course a certain amount of wealth.)

<u>D'abord</u> pour participer à la vie sociale <u>et</u> <u>puis</u> pour améliorer les conditions économiques du foyer. (Not only to take part in the life of the community but also to improve the financial condition of the family.)

6.4 Generalization

Überhaupt/ im allgemeinen
Bref/ enfin/ en somme/ d'une manière générale
(On the whole; In general; Generally speaking; In short)

Das ist kein Vorwurf an die Ärzte, das ist kein Vorwurf an die Pfleger, das ist ein Vorwurf an den Staat und die Gesellschaft im allgemeinen. (I am not criticizing the doctors, I am not criticizing the nurses, I am criticizing the state and society in general.)

Ich habe gelernt, mich zu behaupten, und überhaupt selbständig zu sein. (I have learned to assert myself and on the whole to be independent.)

Il fallait balayer, passer les rouleaux, faire les shampooings, tout quoi...en somme un travail complètement abrutissant. (I had to sweep the floor, pass the rollers, do the shampoos, everything--in short, really dull work.)

6.5 Mitigating

Das heißt/ beziehungsweise/ ich meine
Disons/ à vrai dire/ ou plutôt/ ou si vous préférez/
c'est-à-dire/ enfin
(That is; i.e.; let's say; or rather; I guess)

Der Volkswagen ist ein praktischer Wagen, das heißt für den Stadtverkehr, nicht für lange Strecken. (The VW is a practical car, for city traffic, that is, not for long distances.)

Moi avec mes clientes on se reçoit très souvent--disons qu'elles me reçoivent très souvent chez elles. (My clients and I, we invite each other quite frequently--let's say, they invite me quite frequently to their homes.)

6.6 Restricting

Andererseits/ allerdings/ dagegen/ aber immerhin/ jedoch/ doch

Il est vrai que/ il faut dire que/ évidemment/ cependant/ pourtant/ d'autre part/ néanmoins/ en revanche

(On the other hand; at the same time; although I must say; however; nevertheless; yet)

Die Übersetzungsmethode ist in den Hintergrund getreten, ist allerdings noch nicht ganz verschwunden. (The translation approach is not used as much any more, although I must say, it has not yet completely disappeared.)

J'ai rencontré pas mal de femmes qui s'intéressent à la politique mais néanmoins on rencontre peut-être quand même

moins de femmes que d'hommes qui prennent parti pour les
problèmes politiques. (I have met quite a few women
interested in politics; nevertheless there might be fewer
women than men who actively take part in political issues.)

6.7 Contrasting both sides

Einerseits...andererseits/ auf der einen Seite...auf der
anderen Seite/ zwar...aber

D'un côté...d'un autre côté/ peut-être...n'empêche que/on
dit que...mais en fait (mais en réalité)/ d'une part...
d'autre part

(On the one hand...on the other hand; it is true that...
however)

Der VW Käfer ist zwar praktisch, aber schön ist er nicht.
(The VW bug is practical, but you can't say it is
beautiful.)

Paris n'est peut-être pas la France, mais n'empêche que tout
le monde veut venir travailler à Paris. (It is true that
Paris is not the whole of France; however, everyone wants to
work in Paris.)

6.8 Examining causes

- Es ist ___ deshalb so, weil
- Es hat ___ damit zu tun, daß
o Es ist ___ aus dem Grunde so, weil
o Es liegt ___ daran, daß
o Es kommt ___ daher, daß
o Es hängt ___ damit zusammen, daß
+ Es rührt ___ daher, daß
+ Es ist ___ auf die Tatsache zurückzuführen, daß
+ Der Grund, warum...liegt ___ darin, daß
+ Der Grund, warum...ist ___ der:

(Possible modifiers: sicher/ nämlich/ zum Teil/ zum großen
Teil/ im Grunde/ einfach/ eigentlich/ vor allem/ vor allen
Dingen/ wohl/ nur/ doch nur/ gerade/ vielleicht/
offensichtlich/ natürlich/ irgendwie/ wahrscheinlich)

- Ca explique ___ pourquoi
- Ca tient ___ au fait que
- Ca vient ___ du fait que
- C'est ___ pourquoi
o C'est ___ la raison pour laquelle
o C'est ___ une des raisons pour lesquelles

o   C'est ___ dû au fait que
+   La raison en est ___ la suivante:

(Possible modifiers: sûrement/ bien/ en partie/ en grande
partie/ au fond/ tout simplement/ en fait/ surtout/ avant
tout/ probablement/ uniquement/ bien sûr/ bien entendu/
apparemment/ évidemment/ quand même)

(This is ___ due to the fact that; One of the reasons for
this is ___ that; This is ___ the reason why; This is ___
why)

(Possible modifiers: surely/ namely/ partly/ basically/
simply/ actually/ in fact/ mainly/ primarily/ only/
precisely/ possibly/ obviously/ of course/ somehow/
probably)

6.9 Examining consequences/Drawing conclusions

-   Und da...ja/ also/ eben/ natürlich
o   Also (+ verb)
+   Und infolgedessen

-   Alors évidemment
o   (Et) Donc
o   (Et) Par conséquent

(As a result; consequently; accordingly; therefore; so)

Meine Eltern verstehen sich, <u>also</u> sind da geringe
Reibungsflächen. (My parents get along well, so there are
few conflicts.)

Er ist gestern nicht gekommen, und <u>da</u> weiß ich <u>ja</u> Bescheid.
(He didn't come yesterday, so I've got the message.)

On entend parler de soirées où on dépense des sommes folles.
Il y a <u>donc</u> bien des gens qui gagnent des sommes extrava-
gantes. (You hear of parties for which people spend enormous sums of money, so there must be people who earn
enormous sums of money!)

7. Announcing Several Points

o   Zuerst mal...dann...schließlich
o   Erstens...zweitens
o   Aus zwei Gründen:
+   Zweierlei:

-   Primo...secundo

o   D'abord...ensuite...enfin
o   Premièrement...deuxièmement
o   Pour deux raisons:
o   Il y a deux choses:

(First...then...finally; first...second; for two reasons;
two things:)

8. Adding a Point

o   Da möchte ich noch sagen:
o   Ich wollte auch noch sagen:
+   Hinzu kommt noch:
+   Darüber hinaus:
+   Und noch etwas möchte ich hinzufügen:

o   De plus
o   Il faut dire aussi que
+   Il ne faut pas oublier non plus que
+   Il y a aussi la question de
+   Il y a aussi une chose, c'est que
+   J'aimerais ajouter que

(Furthermore; I would like to add one more point; and
another thing:; I might add; I would also like to mention;
not only that, but...)

9. Prefacing New Point

9.1 Objective

o   Es ist ___ so, daß
o   Die Sache/die Frage ist ___ die:
o   Das Problem ist ___ dies:
+   Man muß sich darüber klar sein, daß

(Possible modifiers: doch/ leider/ bei uns/ heutzutage/
nämlich/ tatsächlich/ eben/ nun einmal/ im Grunde/
bekanntlicherweise)

-   Alors voilà:
-   Tenez:
+   Il ne faut pas oublier que
o   Il y a une chose c'est que

(The thing is; It is a fact that; We must realize that)

9.2 Subjective

+   Ich möchte ___ auf folgendes hinweisen:

+ Ich möchte ___ darauf hinweisen, daß
+ Ich habe ___ folgendes festgestellt:

(Possible modifiers: nur/ vor allem/ vor allen Dingen/ im besonderen/ nachdrücklich/ mal hier/ nun/ eigentlich)

+ J'aimerais vous faire remarquer que
+ Je vous signale que

(I would like to point to the fact that/ mention the fact that/ indicate the following fact:)

10. Buying Time

10.1 Embarrassment or hesitation

- Also/ äh
- Irgendwie
- Sag'n wir mal
o Ich meine
o Wie soll ich sagen

- Bon/ euh
- Bon...ben
- Ben, c'est-à-dire que...vous comprenez
o Enfin
o Si vous voulez
o Disons
o Comment dirais-je

(Well, you know; you know what I mean; of course; O.K.; somehow; sort of)

Wenn die Mutter also ihre Tochter lediglich immer fragt also wohin gehst du, was machst du, also ich meine (When the mother, you know, always asks her daughter, you know, where are you going, what are you doing, you know...I mean)

Also ich finde es ist irgendwie sag'n wir mal viel unverständlicher zu lesen also sag'n wir mal es ist schlechter den Gedanken zu bekommen--ja ich meine man muß öfter hinsehen. (Well I find it somehow, let's say, much more difficult to understand, well, say it's more difficult to get the general idea--I mean, you have to look at it over and over again.)

J'pense qu'ici on peut avoir une vie agréable. Enfin, j'veux dire quand je dis agréable, c'est pas du point du vue bien sûr comment dirais-je matériel. (I feel one can live nicely here. Well, you know, I don't mean, of course, how shall I put it, a material well-being.)

79

On est dans un immeuble très bien...bon...ben...il y a pas
de problème. (We are in a very nice apartment building, you
know--no problem.)

10.2 Generalizing

o   Im großen und ganzen
o   Eigentlich
o   Praktisch
o   An sich
o   An und für sich
o   Im Grunde

o   En somme
o   En fait
o   Pratiquement
o   En fin de compte
o   Au fond
o   En définitive

(On the whole; actually; practically; essentially; basically)

10.3 Mitigating

o   Eigentlich
o   Sozusagen
o   In gewisser Weise
o   Gewissermaßen
o   In gewissem Sinne
o   Zum Teil/ teilweise/ zum großen Teil

o   Pour ainsi dire
o   Si vous voulez
o   En quelque sorte
o   D'un certain côté
o   Dans un certain sens

(Rather; so to speak; more or less; practically; actually)

10.4 Summing up

-   ...oder so (was)
-   ...und so

-   ...et tout (et tout)
-   ...enfin tout (quoi)

(and all that; or anything)

Ich bin nicht krank oder so. (I am not sick or anything.)

Man kann sich unterhalten und so. (You can discuss things and all that.)

Je vais choisir seconde C...enfin tout...quoi. (I will choose a math-oriented 10th grade and all that goes with it.)

11. Guarding against Interruptions

- Moment mal! Einen Moment!
- Lass mich ausreden!
- Ich bin gleich fertig.
+ Darf ich zu Ende reden?

- Une minute!
- Je n'ai pas fini!
- J'ai tout de suite fini.
o Attends, laisse-moi terminer.

(Just a minute; Let me finish; I'm just about to finish; I haven't finished; Wait, let me finish)

12. Returning to the Point (after interruption)

- Wo war ich stehengeblieben?
o (Also) wie gesagt
o Wie ich vorhin (eben) schon sagte
o Jedenfalls:
o Um auf (+ accusative) zurückzukommen:

- Où est-ce que j'en étais?
o Comme je disais tout à l'heure
o En tous cas
o Donc...pour en revenir à ce qu'on disait
+ Quoi qu'il en soit

(Where was I? As I said; In any case; To get back to)

Linking to Partner's Point

13. Restating

13.1 Summing up a point

Also/ mit anderen Worten/ du meinst:
Donc/ autrement dit/ si j'ai bien compris/ d'après vous
(So; What you're saying is; In other words; You mean then;
If I understand you correctly)

Sie würden also nicht in einer Kommune leben wollen. (So you wouldn't want to live in a commune.)

81

Donc le soir vous préférez rester chez vous. (So, evenings you prefer to stay home.)

13.2 Repeating an utterance verbatim

See 5.6.

13.3 Partial or total repetition

Ob ich in einer Kommune leben möchte? Ich? In einer Kommune? (You're asking me if I'd like to live in a commune? Me? In a commune?)

Quels conseils donnez-vous aux jeunes?--Les conseils? Eh bien, des conseils de tout ordre. (What advice do you give young people?--Advice? Well, all kinds of advice.)

14. Cross-Referring to a Previous Point

14.1 To take the floor

```
o    Ich möchte auf das zurückkommen,      ⎫
-    Ich möchte etwas sagen zu dem,        ⎬   Was X vorhin sagte.
+    Ich möchte Bezug nehmen auf das,      ⎪
+    Ich möchte anknüpfen an das,          ⎭
```

- On pourrait revenir une minute à ce que X disait tout à l'heure.
- o Je voudrais revenir sur la question soulevée tout à l'heure.
- + Excusez-moi, mais j'aimerais qu'on revienne.

(I'd like to get back to a point made earlier/to a point you raised earlier.)

14.2 To keep the floor

- Wie du eben gesagt hast
- o Wie X schon sagte
- + Wie X schon angedeutet hat

- Comme tu le disais tout à l'heure
- o Comme X l'a déjà fait remarquer
- o Comme X le mentionnait tout à l'heure

(As you just said; As X suggested; As X said)

15. Piggy-Backing

15.1 To elaborate on a previous point

o   Zu diesem/dem Punkt,
o   In dieser Beziehung,   }   würde ich sagen:
+   In dieser Hinsicht,

+   A ce propos,
+   A ce sujet,   }   j'aimerais ajouter que
+   A cet égard,

(In this respect; With regard to..., I would like to say/
add)

15.2 With assent/dissent + comment

-    Das ist es ja gerade!
o   Das finde ich sehr interessant und zwar:
+   Das würde ich sehr unterstreichen:

-    C'est justement ça!
o   C'est un point très important:
+   C'est un point que j'aimerais souligner.

(That's just it. This is a very interesting point. That is
a very important point.)

15.3 To bring in an additional point

-    Es kommt ja auch noch eine Sache dazu:
o   Da kommen wir eigentlich auf die Frage:
o   Ein zweites Problem ist natürlich auch:
+   Da kommt etwas sehr Wichtiges hinzu:

o   Ca pose évidemment le problème de
-    Il y a aussi une autre chose, c'est que
+   Ca nous amène à considérer
+   Il y a aussi quelque chose qu'il ne faut pas oublier:

(That raises the question of; This brings up another point/
leads to another important question:)

16. Counter-Argument

16.1 With concession

-    Ja gut/ schön/ mag sein/ das gebe ich zu/ das kann
natürlich sein/ sicher/ es ist natürlich richtig...bloß
ich meine/ aber ich meine/ aber immerhin

+ Eins ist richtig:/ es mag (durchaus) sein, daß/ ich gebe
dir soweit recht, daß/ ich möchte nicht bestreiten, daß
...auf der anderen Seite (verb)/ andererseits/ aber man
müßte auch sagen:/ aber ich möchte eines bestreiten:

- Bon/ oui/ d'accord/ c'est possible/ effectivement/ je
veux bien/ si vous voulez/ admettons...mais/ quand même/
n'empêche que

+ Il est certain que/ il est exact que/ je reconnais que
tu as raison:/ je ne nie pas que...mais cependant/ mais
pourtant/ cela n'empêche pas que/ mais néanmoins

(O.K./ Granted; That's possible/ Sure/ Of course you're
right...but still/ but I mean/ but nevertheless it is possible that/ One thing is correct/ I grant you that/ I don't
deny that/...but on the other hand/ but still you have to
admit/ but one would have to say/ but I will deny that)

16.2 Without concession

- Es tut mir leid, aber
- Entschuldigung, aber
+ Es geht hier nicht um...sondern um
+ Es handelt sich nicht um...sondern um

o Je regrette, mais
o Ah pardon, mais
+ Il ne s'agit pas de ça:

(I'm sorry/excuse me, but...; that's not the point; It's
not a question of...but of)

Responding (Back-Channel Activities)

17. Asking for Clarification (for repair purposes)

17.1 On the general point

- Wieso (eigentlich) (denn) das?
- Warum (denn) (eigentlich) nicht?

o Je ne vois pas (du tout) pourquoi.
o Je ne vois pas ce que tu veux dire.

(How come? Why is that? I don't see why not.)

17.2 On specific words

- Wieso schädlich?

-   Was meinst du: schädlich?
-   Wie meinst du das?

-   Comment ça "nuisible"?
-   Qu'est-ce que tu veux dire par "nuisible"?
o   Qu'est-ce que cela signifie "nuisible"?

(What do you mean: damaging? What do you mean by that?)

17.3 On the general meaning

o   Wie bitte?
o   Was meinst du (genau)?
-   Wie war das (noch einmal)?
-   Verzeihung, wie war das?
-   Das habe ich nicht mitgekriegt/ Was meintest du?
o   Ich habe das nicht richtig verstanden.
o   Was war mit X?

o   Comment?
o   Qu'est-ce que vous dites?
o   Pardon, vous dites?
o   Vous voulez répéter s'il vous plaît?
o   Je n'ai pas compris, vous pourriez répéter s.v.p.?
o   Qu'est-ce que tu veux dire par là?

(Excuse me, what was that? I didn't get that, could you
repeat it? What do you mean exactly? What was that about
X?)

18. Acknowledgment

18.1 General

-   Ja.
-   Was?
-   Ach so/ So.
-   Wirklich? Tatsächlich? Tatsache?
-   Na und?

-   Oui.
-   Quoi?
-   Ah bon.
-   Vraiment? C'est vrai? C'est pas vrai!
-   Ah, d'accord.

(Yes. What? Aha! Really? Honestly? No kidding. So what!)

18.2 Specific

(With repetition in interrogative form of single elements of
the point made previously. See 13.3.)

19. Assent

19.1 Objective

-   (Ja) Genau!
-   (Ist doch) Klar!
-   Unbedingt!
-   Ja eben! Eben! Na eben! Das ist es eben!
-   's stimmt!
-   Sicher!
- o   Das ist richtig.
- o   Völlig richtig.
- o   So ist es!
- o   Das habe ich ja gesagt.
- o   Das kann man wohl sagen.

-   (Oui) C'est ça!
-   Voilà!/ D'accord!
-   Absolument!
-   Tout juste!
-   En effet!
- o   C'est certain.
- o   C'est justement (ça).
- o   C'est l'évidence même.
- o   C'est ce que je disais.

(Right! You're right! That's for sure! That's exactly it!
Exactly! That's it! That's just it! That's true! Sure!
You've got a point there! That's a good point! That's a good
question! You can say that again!)

19.2 Subjective

-   Das finde ich auch./ Das glaube ich auch.
- o   Ich bin ganz deiner Meinung.
- o   Ich stimme vollkommen/völlig/durchaus mit dir überein.
- o   Du hast völlig/vollkommen/ganz recht.
- o   Da gebe ich dir vollkommen recht.
- +   Ich stimme dir da völlig zu.

-   Je suis complètement/totalement/tout à fait/absolument
  d'accord avec toi.
- o   C'est justement ce que je voulais dire.
-   Je trouve aussi.
- o   Tu as parfaitement/totalement/tout à fait raison.
- o   Je suis du même avis.

(I totally/fully/completely agree. I feel the same way.
I share your opinion. That's exactly the way I feel about
it.)

19.3 Giving in

- Na ja, es kann sein.
- Also gut.
- Gut, also dann.
- Na schön.
o Meinetwegen (also).
o (Also) Da sind wir uns einig.

- Bon, je veux bien.
- Bon, c'est d'accord.
- Bon, si tu veux.
- On est d'accord.
- Peut-être bien.

(Well, O.K. All right. It's all right with me. We both
agree.)

20. Dissent

20.1 Objective

- Das ist (ja) nicht wahr!
- Das ist ja Unsinn!
- Das ist doch gar nicht drin/ganz unmöglich.
- Das ist ganz was anderes.
- Es hat damit nichts zu tun.
- Das sagst du!
o Das stimmt ja gar nicht.
o Darauf kommt es gar nicht an.
+ Das ist (durchaus) nicht der Fall.

- C'est faux!
- Jamais de la vie!
- Mais ce n'est pas vrai!
- Ce n'est pas ça.
- Mais absolument pas!
- Bien au contraire!
o C'est tout à fait autre chose.
o Ca n'a rien à voir.
o Ce n'est pas le cas.
o Je ne parle pas de ça.

(That's not true! Come on! That's ridiculous! No way!
That's beside the point. This is totally irrelevant. This
just isn't the case. That's what you say!)

20.2 Subjective

- Das glaube ich/finde ich gar nicht/absolut nicht/ganz und gar nicht/überhaupt nicht/eben gar nicht.
- Ich bin gar nicht deiner Meinung/der Meinung.
- o Ich stimme nicht mit dir überein.
- o Da bin ich ganz anderer Meinung/anderer Ansicht.
- o Ich habe meine Bedenken.
- + Das bezweifle ich (eben).
- + Das möchte ich unheimlich bezweifeln.

- Je ne trouve pas/pas du tout/absolument pas.
- Je ne suis pas du tout d'accord (avec toi).
- Je suis contre.
- Je ne suis pas du tout du même avis.
- o Moi, j'ai mes doutes.
- o J'en doute.
- + Je suis tout à fait d'un autre avis/d'avis contraire.

(I don't believe that. I don't feel that way at all. I don't agree at all. I have quite a different opinion/view of things. I have my doubts. I doubt that very much.)

21. Noncommittal

21.1 Indecision

- Tja, das ist (ja) (eben) die Frage.
- o Das ist (aber) gerade das Problem.
- o Ich weiß nicht, was ich davon halten soll/darüber denken soll.

- Ben, c'est vraiment là la question.
- o C'est précisément ça la question.
- o Je ne sais pas quoi en penser.

(That's a good question. Well, that's precisely the question. I don't know what to think. I'm really not sure what to think.)

21.2 Mitigation

- Das würde ich nicht sagen.
- o Nun, es kommt darauf an (wie man die Sache betrachtet).
- o Man kann es auch anders betrachten.
- + Das eine schließt das andere nicht aus.

- Ca dépend.
- o Tout dépend de ce que
- o L'un n'empêche pas l'autre.
- o Je n'irais pas aussi loin.

(Well, it depends how you look at it. You can look at it
this way. I wouldn't say that. You can look at it both
ways.)

22. Fighting Back

- So habe ich das gar nicht gemeint!
- Das habe ich (aber) auch nicht gesagt!
+ Das bestreite ich ja gar nicht!

- Mais je n'ai jamais dit ça!
+ Ne me faites pas dire ce que je n'ai pas dit!

(That's not what I said! That's not what I meant! I don't
deny that! Don't put words into my mouth!)

NOTES

1. The taxonomy proposed by the T-level for English was
greatly expanded for French by the CREDIF team. See D. Coste et
al., 1976, Un Niveau seuil (Strasbourg: Council of Europe),
ED 168 344.

2. See G. Neuner, R. Schmidt, H. Wilms and M. Zirkel, 1979,
Deutsch Aktiv I. Ein Lehrwerk für Erwachsene; and G. Neuner,
R. Schmidt, H. Wilms, C. Edelhoff, J. Gerighausen and T. Scher-
ling, 1980, Deutsch Aktiv II (München: Langenscheidt). Also
R. Schäpers, R. Luscher and M. Glück, 1980, Grundkurs Deutsch
(München: Verlag für Deutsch). See also the many activities
centered around speech functions for communicative language
teaching suggested in W. Rivers, 1975, Autonomous interaction
(Chapter 2 of A practical guide to the teaching of French/Ger-
man/Spanish (Oxford University Press); C. Edelhoff et al., 1978,
Kommunikativer Englischunterricht, Prinzipien und Übungstypol-
ogie (München: Langenscheidt-Longman) (in preparation for the
teaching of German); A. Maley and A. Duff, 1978, Drama techniques in language learning (Cambridge University Press); Fiusa,
Kehl and Weiss, 1978, En effeuillant la marguerite (Chicago:
Langenscheidt-Hachette); G. Vigner, 1979, Parler et convaincre
(Paris: Hachette).

3. See A. Davison and P. Gordon, 1978, Games and simulations in action (London: The Woburn Press) and A. Omaggio,
1978, Games and simulations in the foreign language classroom
(Arlington, VA: Center for Applied Linguistics/ERIC Clearinghouse on Languages and Linguistics), ED 177 887. Some of the
activities described in the sections on "Learning Conversational
Management" and "Debates and Discussions" are adaptations of
Fiusa, Kehl and Weiss, 1978, En effeuillant la marguerite
(Chicago: Langenscheidt-Hachette); G. Vigner, 1979, Parler et
convaincre (Paris: Hachette); I. Spiegelman, 1980, Spiel im
Fremdsprachenunterricht, Newsletter on Education 4 (12) (New
York: Goethe Institute); C. Kell and J. Winn, 1976, Teaching
public speaking with simulations, ED 127 647; E. Keller and
S. Warner, 1976, Gambits 1-3: A course for teaching English to
adult francophones in the Public Service of Canada (Ottawa:
Public Service Commission), ED 154 611-613. The game of per-
suasion on p. 54, "Hard Sell," was the idea of my colleague
Frederic Hodgson.

4. <u>Inter</u> <u>Nationes</u>, kultureller Tonbanddienst. Kennedy Allee 91-103, D5300 Bonn-Bad Godesberg. The following are useful at the intermediate level:
Audiovisuelles Ergänzungsmaterial zur Landeskunde der Bundesrepublik Deutschland

* Modell 1: Sprach- und Hörverstehensübungen
* Modell 2: Sprechsituationen aus dem Alltag
* Modell 3: Themengebundene Hörverstehensübungen: Schule, Universität, Beruf
* Modell 4: Sprechsituationen in Auswahl
* Modell 5: Weitere Sprechsituationen aus dem Alltag
* Modell 6: Themen und Meinungen im Für und Wider

Bureau pour l'Enseignement de la Langue et de la Civilisation Française à l'Etranger: <u>Langue</u> <u>et</u> <u>Civilisation</u>: 12 dossiers pour la classe avec exploitation de documents sonores. Niveaux I et II.

J. Frommer and M. Weitz, 1979, <u>Femmes</u> <u>et</u> <u>métiers</u> (Modern Language Center, Harvard University.) (Includes tapes, transcriptions, and background information.)

5. Interview by Irmgard Hicks, Goethe Institute, 1975.

6. Passage from Judith G. Frommer and Margaret C. Weitz, 1979, "Betty Baed, coiffeuse," <u>Femmes</u> <u>et</u> <u>métiers</u> (Cambridge, MA: Modern Language Center, Harvard University, 1979). Reprinted with permission of the authors.

BIBLIOGRAPHY

Allen, J.P.B. and H.G. Widdowson. 1974. Teaching the communi-
cative use of English. In International Review of Applied
Linguistics in Language Teaching 12 (1): 1-21.
Austin, J.L. 1962. How to do things with words. Oxford:
Clarendon Press.
Baird, C.A. 1965. Rhetoric: A philosophical inquiry. New
York: Ronald Press.
Bellack, A.A., H.M. Kliebard, R.T. Hyman, and F.L. Smith. 1966.
The language of the classroom. New York: Teachers College
Press.
Burton, D. 1980. Dialogue and discourse: A sociolinguistic
approach to modern drama dialogue and naturally-occurring
conversation. London: Routledge and Keagan Paul.
Candlin, C.N. 1976. Communicative language teaching and the
debt to pragmatics. In Semantics: Theory and application,
Clea Rameh, ed. Georgetown University Round Table on Lan-
guages and Linguistics, 1976. Washington, DC: Georgetown
University Press.
_____ and M.P. Breen. 1981. Discourse analysis, psychological
processes and designing exercise types for language learning.
Workshop presented at TESOL annual meeting.
Chomsky, N. 1957. Syntactic structures. The Hague: Mouton.
Coulthard, M. 1977. An introduction to discourse analysis.
London: Longman.
Debyser, F. 1978. L'expression du désaccord en français.
Paris: Bureau pour l'Enseignement de la Langue et de la
Civilisation Française à l'Etranger.
Dore, J. 1974. A pragmatic description of early language
development. Journal of Psycholinguistic Research 3: 343-50.
_____. 1975. Holophrases, speech acts and language universals.
Journal of Child Language 2: 21-39.
Ferguson, J. 1975. Interruptions in spontaneous dialogue.
(as cited in Coulthard, pp. 57 and 61).
Fillmore, C.J. 1972. May we come in. In Sociolinguistics in
cross-cultural perspective, D.M. Smith and R.W. Shuy, eds.
Washington, DC: Georgetown University Press.
Fillmore, L.W. 1979. Individual differences in second language
acquisition. In Individual differences in second language
ability and language behavior, C.J. Fillmore and W.S.Y. Wang,
eds. New York: Academic Press.

Firth, J.R. 1964. On sociological linguistics. In Language in culture and society: A reader in linguistics and anthropology, D. Hymes, ed. New York: Harper & Row.

Fraser, B. 1979. Research in pragmatics in second language acquisition: The state of the art. Paper presented at annual TESOL meeting, Boston.

Frommer, J.G. and W. Ishikawa. 1980. Alors...euh...on parle français? The French Review 53 (4): 501-6.

Frommer, J.G. and M.C. Weitz. 1979. Femmes et métiers. Cambridge, MA: Modern Language Center, Harvard University.

Garvey, C. 1975. Requests and responses in children's speech. Journal of Child Language 2: 41-63.

_____. 1977. The contingent query: A dependent act in conversation. In Interaction, conversation and the development of language, L.M. and L.A. Rosenblum, eds. New York: John Wiley.

Goodwin, C. 1975. The interactive construction of the sentence within the turn at talk in natural conversation. Paper presented at the annual meeting of the American Anthropological Association, San Francisco.

Gordon, D. and G. Lakoff. 1971. Conversational postulates. In Papers from the seventh regional meeting of the Chicago Linguistic Society. Chicago: C.L.S.

Gremmo, M.J. et al. 1977. Interactional structure: The role of role. Mélanges pédagogiques. Université de Nancy, Centre de Recherches et d'Applications Pédagogiques en Langues. ED 149 626.

Grice, H. 1975. Logic and conversation. In Syntax and semantics, vol. 3, speech acts, P. Cole and J. Morgan, eds. New York: Academic Press.

Grimes, J.E. 1975. The thread of discourse. The Hague, Paris: Mouton.

Halliday, M.A.K. 1973. Explorations in the functions of language. London: Arnold.

_____. 1975. Learning how to mean. London: Arnold.

Hatch, E. 1978. Discourse analysis and second language acquisition. In Second language acquisition: A book of readings, E. Hatch, ed. Rowley, MA: Newbury House.

Heath, S.B. 1978. Teacher talk: Language in the classroom. Language in Education series, No. 9. Arlington, VA: Center for Applied Linguistics/ERIC Clearinghouse on Languages and Linguistics. ED 158 575.

Holec, H. 1974. L'illocution: Problématique et méthodologie. In Linguistic insights in applied linguistics, 2d Neuchatel Colloquium in Applied Linguistics, S.P. Corder and E. Roulet, eds. Paris: Didier.

_____. 1979. Autonomy and foreign language learning. Strasbourg: Council of Europe. ED 192 557.

Hymes, D. 1964. Introduction: Toward ethnographies of communication. In The ethnography of communication, J.J. Gumperz and D. Hymes, eds. American Anthropologist 66 (6).

Hymes, D. 1971. Sociolinguistics and the ethnography of speaking. In Social anthropology and linguistics, E. Ardener, ed. Association of Social Anthropologists, Monograph 10. London: Tavistock.

_____. 1972a. Models of the interaction of language and social life. In Directions in sociolinguistics, J.J. Gumperz and D. Hymes, eds. New York: Holt, Rinehart & Winston.

_____. 1972b. On communicative competence. In Sociolinguistics, J.B. Pride and J. Holmes, eds. Harmondsworth: Penguin.

Jäger, K-H. 1976a. Zur Argumentation in Texten gesprochener Sprache. Deutschunterricht 28 (4): 59-71.

_____. 1976b. Zur Beendigung von Dialogen. In Heutiges Deutsch I/12 Projekt Dialogstrukturen. Ein Arbeitsbericht, F.J. Berens, K-H. Jäger, G. Schank, and J. Schwitalla, eds. München: Max Hueber.

Jefferson, G. 1972. Side sequences. In Studies in social interaction, D. Sudnow, ed. New York: The Free Press.

_____. 1973. A case of precision timing in ordinary conversation: Overlapped tag-positioned address terms in closing sequences. Semiotica 9 (1): 47-96.

Johns, T.F. 1974. Seminar discourse strategies: Problems and principles in role-simulation. In Pariser Werkstattgespräche. Laborübungen für Fortgeschrittene. München: Goethe-Institut.

Jorstad, H. 1974. Testing as communication. In The challenge of communication, G.A. Jarvis, ed. ACTFL Foreign Language Education Series, Vol. 6. Skokie, IL: National Textbook Company.

Keenan, E.O. 1975. Conversational competence in children. Journal of Child Language 1 (2): 163-83.

_____. and E. Klein. 1975. Coherency in children's discourse. Journal of Psycholinguistic Research 4 (4): 365-80.

Kelly, G.A. 1963. A theory of personality- Psychology of personal constructs. New York: Norton.

Krashen, S. 1978. The monitor model for second language acquisition. In Second language acquisition and foreign language teaching, R.C. Gingràs, ed. Arlington, VA: Center for Applied Linguistics.

Labov, W. 1970. The study of language in its social context. Studium Generale 23: 30-87.

_____. 1972. Rules for ritual insults. In Studies in social interaction, D. Sudnow, ed. New York: Free Press.

Larsen-Freeman, D. 1980. Discourse analysis in second language research. Rowley, MA: Newbury House.

Oller, J.W., Jr. 1970. Linguistics and the pragmatics of communication. ED 041 292.

_____. 1973. Focus on the learner: Pragmatic perspectives for the foreign language teacher. Rowley, MA: Newbury House.

Omaggio, A.C. 1978. Games and simulations in the foreign language classroom. Language in Education series, No. 13.

Arlington, VA: Center for Applied Linguistics/ERIC Clearinghouse on Languages and Linguistics. ED 177 887.

Peck, S. 1978. Child-child discourse in second language acquisition. In Second language acquisition: A book of readings,
E. Hatch, ed. Rowley, MA: Newbury House.

Perelman, C. 1970. Traité de l'argumentation. La nouvelle
rhétorique. Bruxelles: Institut de Sociologie.

Piaget, J. 1926. The language and thought of the child. New
York: Harcourt Brace.

Portine, H. 1978. Apprendre à argumenter. Analyse de discours
et didactique des langues. Paris: Bureau pour l'Enseignement de la Langue et de la Civilisation Française à
l'Etranger.

Riley, P. 1976a. An experiment in teaching communicative competence within a restricted discourse. Paper presented at
the Colloquium of the Swiss Interuniversity Commission for
Applied Linguistics. ED 162 539.

_____. 1976b. Discursive and communicative functions of non-
verbal communication. Mélanges pédagogiques. Université de
Nancy, Centre de Recherches et d'Applications Pédagogiques en
Langues. ED 143 217.

_____. 1977. Discourse networks in classroom interaction.
Some problems in communicative language teaching. Mélanges
pédagogiques. Université de Nancy, Centre de Recherches et
d'Applications Pédagogiques en Langues. ED 149 629.

_____. 1979. When communication breaks down: Levels of coher-
ence in discourse. In Applied Linguistics I (3), J. Sinclair,
ed. Oxford: Clarendon Press.

_____. 1980a. Directions in the description of discourse
structure. Paper submitted to the Council for Cultural
Cooperation of the Council of Europe, March-April 1980.

_____. 1980b. Mud and stars: Sensitization, personal con-
structs and learning. Paper presented at the Bern Colloquium
on Applied Linguistics, June 1980.

Rivers, W.M. 1973. From linguistic competence to communicative
competence. TESOL Quarterly 7 (1): 25-34.

Sacks, H. 1972. An initial investigation of the usability of
conversational data for doing sociology. In Studies in
social interaction, D. Sudnow, ed. New York: The Free
Press.

_____ and E.A. Schegloff. 1974. Two preferences in the organization of reference to persons in conversation and their
interaction. In Ethnomethodology, labelling and deviant
behavior, N. Avison and R. Wilson, eds. London: Routledge
and Kegan Paul.

Sacks, H., E.A. Schegloff, and G. Jefferson. 1974. A simplest
systematics for the organization of turn-taking for conversation. Language 50 (4): 696-735.

Sajavaara, K. and J. Lehtonen. 1978. Spoken language and the
concept of fluency. ED 158 600.

Sajavaara, K. and J. Lehtonen. 1980. Papers in discourse and contrastive discourse analysis. Reports from the Department of English, University of Jyväskylä, No. 6. Jyväskylä Contrastive Studies, No. 5. Jyväskylä, Finland: Language Centre for Finnish Universities. FL 012 297.

Sajavaara, K. and J. Lehtonen. 1980. The analysis of cross-language communication: Prolegomena to the theory and methodology. In Towards a cross-linguistic assessment of speech production, H. Dechert and M. Raupach, eds. Bern: Lang.

Schegloff, E.A. 1968. Sequencing in conversational openings. American Anthropologist 70 (6): 1075-95.

_____. 1972. Notes on a conversational practice: Formulating place. In Studies in social interaction, D. Sudnow, ed. New York: Free Press.

Schwartz, J.L. 1977. Repair in conversations between adult second language learners of English. ED 162 540.

Scollon, R.T. 1973. A real early stage: An unzippered condensation of a dissertation on child language. University of Hawaii Working Papers in Linguistics 5: 67-81. ED 094 561.

Searle, J.R. 1969. Speech acts. London: Cambridge University Press.

Sinclair, J.McH., ed. 1980. Applied Linguistics I (3). Special issue on discourse analysis. Oxford: Clarendon Press.

_____ and R.M. Coulthard. 1975. Towards an analysis of discourse. The English used by teachers and pupils. London: Oxford University Press.

Stubbs, M. (Forthcoming.) Discourse analysis: The sociolinguistic analysis of natural conversation. London: Blackwell.

Valette, R.M. 1973. Developing and evaluating communication skills in the classroom. TESOL Quarterly 7 (4): 407.

Widdowson, H.G. 1973. An applied linguistic approach to discourse analysis. Ph.D. dissertation, University of Edinburgh.

Wilkins, D. 1972a. An investigation into the linguistic and situational context of the common core in a unit/credit system. Strasbourg: Council of Europe. ED 082 545.

_____. 1972b. Grammatical, situational and notional syllabuses. Proceedings from the Third Congress of Applied Linguistics, Copenhagen. ED 136 549.

Most documents identified by an ED number may be read on microfiche at an ERIC library collection or ordered from the ERIC Document Reproduction Service, P.O. Box 190, Arlington, VA 22210. Ordering information for all those ED-numbered documents not available directly through the ERIC system can be found in the ERIC monthly abstract journal, Resources in Education. Documents with FL numbers are being processed by EDRS and will be assigned ED numbers upon announcement in Resources in Education.

Claire Kramsch (Diplômée de l'Université de Paris) is senior
lecturer and coordinator of German studies in the foreign languages and literatures section of the department of humanities
at the Massachusetts Institute of Technology. She has presented
papers and given workshops on communication and second language
teaching at the conferences of the American Association of Teachers of German, the Massachusetts Foreign Language Association,
the Massachusetts Association of Teachers of English to Speakers
of Other Languages, the American Council on the Teaching of
Foreign Languages, the Internationaler Deutschlehrerverband and
the Goethe Institute. Her articles have appeared in Unterrichts-
praxis, the AATF Bulletin, Foreign Language Annals, Zielsprache
Deutsch, and Goethe-Institut Werkstattgespräche.

LANGUAGE IN EDUCATION: THEORY AND PRACTICE

The Language in Education series can be purchased by volume or by
individual titles. The subscription rate is $32.00 per volume
for Volumes 1 and 2; $37.00 for Volume 3; and $47.00 for Volume
4. Add $1.75 postage and handling charges for individual orders.
D.C. residents add 6% sales tax. ALL ORDERS MUST BE PREPAID. To
subscribe to the complete series of publications, write to:

Publications Department
Center for Applied Linguistics
3520 Prospect Street NW
Washington DC 20007

Below is a selected list of series titles:

Volume 1 (1977-78)

6. From the Community to the Classroom: Gathering Second-
   Language Speech Samples, by Barbara F. Freed. $2.95.
   ED 157 404
7. Kinesics and Cross-Cultural Understanding, by Genelle G.
   Morain. $2.95. ED 157 405
8. New Perspectives on Teaching Vocabulary, by Howard H. Keller.
   $2.95. ED 157 406
9. Teacher Talk: Language in the Classroom, by Shirley B. Heath.
   $2.95. ED 158 575
10. Language and Linguistics: Bases for a Curriculum, by Julia S.
    Falk. $2.95. ED 158 576
11. Teaching Culture: Strategies and Techniques, by Robert C.
    Lafayette. $2.95. ED 157 407
12. Personality and Second Language Learning, by Virginia D.
    Hodge. $2.95. ED 157 408

Volume 2 (1978-79)

13. Games and Simulations in the Foreign Language Classroom, by
    Alice C. Omaggio. $5.95. ED 177 887
16. Foreign Languages, English as a Second/Foreign Language, and
    the U.S. Multinational Corporation, by Marianne Inman.
    $4.95. ED 179 089
17. Testing Oral Communication in the Foreign Language Classroom,
    by Walter H. Bartz. $2.95. ED 176 590
18. Intensive Foreign Language Courses, by David P. Benseler and
    Renate A. Schulz. $4.95. ED 176 587
19. Evaluating a Second Language Program, by Gilbert A. Jarvis
    and Shirley J. Adams. $2.95. ED 176 589
20. Reading a Second Language, by G. Truett Cates and Janet K.
    Swaffar. $2.95. ED 176 588

Volume 3 (1979-80)

24. Testing in Foreign Languages, ESL, and Bilingual Education, 1966-1979: A Select, Annotated ERIC Bibliography, compiled by Dale L. Lange and Ray T. Clifford. $7.95. ED 183 027
25. ACTFL 1979: Abstracts of Presented Papers. $5.95. ED 183 031
26. A Guide to Language Camps in the United States, by Lois Vines. $3.95. ED 183 030
28. Teaching a Second Language: A Guide for the Student Teacher, by Constance K. Knop. $4.95. ED 195 165
29. Assessing Study Abroad Programs for Secondary School Students, by Helene Z. Loew. $2.95. ED 193 974
30. Chinese Language Study in American Higher Education: State of the Art, by Peter A. Eddy, James J. Wrenn, and Sophia A. Behrens. $7.95. ED 195 166
31. Sentence Combining in Second Language Instruction, by Thomas C. Cooper, Genelle Morain, and Theodore Kalivoda. $7.95. ED 195 167
32. Teaching the Metric System in the Foreign Language Classroom, by Bette Le Feber Stevens. $4.95. ED 195 168

Volume 4 (1980-81)

33. Directory of Foreign Language Service Organizations: 2, by Sophia A. Behrens. $7.00.
34. The Older Foreign Language Learner: A Challenge for Colleges and Universities, by Elizabeth G. Joiner. $4.00.
36. Helping Learners Succeed: Activities for the Foreign Language Classroom, by Alice C. Omaggio. $5.00.
39. Teaching French as a Multicultural Language: The French-Speaking World Outside of Europe, by John D. Ogden. $4.50.
40. PR Prototypes: A Guidebook for Promoting Foreign Language Study to the Public, by Rosanne G. Royer and Lester W. McKim. $7.00.